M000013947

Presented to:

_____

From:

_____

Date:

_____

SOUL
SANCTUARY
FINDING YOUR PLACE OF PEACE

HONOR BOOKS

Inspiration and Motivation for the Seasons of Life

An Imprint of Cook Communications Ministries • Colorado Springs, CO

10 09 08 07 06 05   10 9 8 7 6 5 4 3 2 1

Soul Sanctuary—Finding Your Place of Peace
ISBN#   1-56292-219-X

Copyright © 2005 Bordon Books
6532 E. 71st Street, Suite 105
Tulsa, OK 74133

Published by Honor Books,
An Imprint of Cook Communications Ministries
4050 Lee Vance View
Colorado Springs, CO 80918

Developed by Bordon Books

Manuscript written by Edna G. Jordan
Cover designed by LJ Designs

Printed in Canada. All rights reserved under
International Copyright Law. Contents and/or cover
may not be reproduced in whole or in part in any form
without the express written consent of the Publisher.

INTRODUCTION

Do you wish for a place to lay down your worries and troubles? Do you long to feel that someone else will take care of the problems that you are unable to control? *Soul Sanctuary* can help you experience God's peace and teach you to trust in God to provide solutions. God can lead you to a place where you can breathe easy and relax. Then you can take that peace out into your world and into the lives of your loved ones.

This book of reflections will help you find the sanctuary that your soul craves. You may believe that you cannot stop worrying, but God provides meditations of peace in the Bible to counterattack the assault on your tranquility.

Soul Sanctuary is filled with powerful devotional insights and Bible verses that demonstrate God's love and faithfulness to you. You will learn how to focus on God's promises of rest and gain courage to face your day in the midst of life's difficulties. Go ahead. Break free from fear, worry, and anxiety. Relax in His presence and rest in His love.

For God hath not given us the spirit of fear;
but of power, and of love, and of a sound mind.

2 TIMOTHY 1:7 KJV

SORRY, WRONG NUMBER

When they call on me, I will answer.

PSALM 91:15 NLT

Often we need information urgently, but we are limited in finding the results we need due to time constraints or miscommunication. Instead of a doctor, we reach an answering service after hours at the pediatrician's office, the church offices are closed for lunch, or information provides the wrong phone number.

Aren't you glad that God does not work on a time clock? That He does not hang out a "Closed" sign at the end of the day or hang up when you call?

The Bible says that God continually watches over you and that He is always awake, waiting to hear from you—no matter what time of day or night. If you have a problem, God is there with comfort and strength. If you have a question, He's waiting with an answer. If you need to talk, God is ready to communicate.

———

GOD IS NEVER CONCERNED ABOUT THE TIME.
HE ALWAYS WANTS TO HEAR FROM YOU.

AGING WITH GRACE

They will still yield fruit in old age;
They shall be full of sap and very green,
To declare that the LORD is upright;
He is my rock.

PSALM 92:14-15 NASB

Have you noticed how much stress we feel about aging? We frantically watch for the inevitable first gray hair and then rush to cover it up. We notice wrinkles and spend loads of money on creams or injections to make them disappear. Too often, we are anxious about signs of aging—energy loss, memory loss, and changes in appearance.

Let it go. The Bible says that God will renew our strength if we wait on Him (Isaiah 40:31). Solomon tells you that gray hair is a badge of honor. (See Proverbs 20:29.) Rest in the truth of God's Word. Think about the important lessons you have learned from life. Every year has been valuable. Would you want to trade one of them for the inexperience of youth?

THE FLAVORS IN CHEESE AND WINE IMPROVE,
DEEPEN, AND BECOME MORE COMPLEX WITH AGE.
THE WORLD'S GREATEST ANTIQUITIES ARE MUTE
TESTIMONIES TO ENDURANCE AND TIMELESS VALUE.
AS YOU MATURE, REMEMBER THAT GOD GIVES HIS
PEOPLE A GLORY AND HONOR THAT FAR SURPASS
ALL OTHERS.

WHAT IF . . . ?

Do not fret or have any anxiety about anything, but in every circumstance and in everything, by prayer and petition (definite requests), with thanksgiving, continue to make your wants known to God.

PHILIPPIANS 4:6 AMP

What are you worried about right now? Chances are your fear is related to the future and what could happen. God does not want you to suffer with an energy level drained by stress and fear. You can let it go. How?

Tell Him about it. Tell Him what you need. Place your fear in His hands. Thank Him ahead of time for taking care of your problems just as you would if a friend volunteered to take care of a heavy task for you—for God does that. When the heavy burden lifts from your shoulders, you will find that God's peace allows you to stop worrying.

———

WHEN YOU WORRY, LET THAT BE A SIGNAL TO
IMMEDIATELY TAKE YOUR FEAR TO GOD.
PLACE IT IN HIS HANDS, SIT BACK, AND RELAX.
HE'LL TAKE CARE OF IT . . . AND YOU.

IT'S TIME TO REST!

"Come to me, all you who are weary and burdened, and I will give you rest. Take my yoke upon you and learn from me, for I am gentle and humble in heart, and you will find rest for your souls."

MATTHEW 11:28-29 NIV

Twenty-four hours is not enough time for all you have to do. Someone or something constantly demands your immediate attention: family, job, church, or another meeting. Thoughts inadvertently cross your mind, interfering with your rest and sleep. You feel stretched thin like a rubber band—about to snap! "Dear Lord, I feel like I'm losing it! Please help me."

Your Heavenly Father waits patiently for your prayer and stands ready to help you. He knows of your busyness, limitations, and need for rest. After creating the universe, God rested. Likewise, God provides for your rest. The psalmist states that "He makes me lie down in [fresh, tender] green pastures; He leads me beside the still and restful waters" (Psalm 23:2 AMP).

Resting in God brings relief and restores your joy, strength, and energy. His rest allows you to truly rejoice and be glad about the new day the Lord has made.

———

THE SWEET QUIETNESS OF GOD'S PRESENCE WASHES AWAY THE STRESS AND EXHAUSTION THAT COME FROM RUNNING ON LIFE'S TREADMILL.

THE PEACE THAT IS DIFFERENT

Peace I leave with you; my peace I give you.
I do not give to you as the world gives.

JOHN 14:27 NIV

The world gives the word peace many meanings. Often, peace refers to a lack of war or noise (something parents dream about!). Peace also refers to the inner quiet that results after a long relaxing day. Although these are all correct definitions of peace, the peace that Jesus gives to those who belong to Him is different.

How is it different? The peace Jesus gives can rule the heart in the midst of war, in the midst of noise, and in the midst of a stressful day because this spiritual peace does not rely on peaceful circumstances. In addition, Jesus promises His peace—the peace He personally experiences. Jesus' peace comes from His knowledge of God's trustworthy character and flawless plan for the universe—and you. When Jesus comes to dwell in your heart, everything that He is becomes available to you, including a peace unlike any the world has ever seen.

GO TO JESUS BEFORE THE DAY STARTS,
HAND OVER YOUR LIFE FOR THAT DAY, AND LET HIM
FILL YOU WITH HIMSELF.

DON'T LOOK BACK!

In your love you kept me from the pit of destruction; you have put all my sins behind your back.

ISAIAH 38:17 NIV

When you run into old friends or go to a class reunion, you probably reminisce about the good old days—the friends, the parties, the fun, and even the trouble you caused. But now that you are a Christian, do you struggle to keep your past in the past? Perhaps you are embarrassed and feel unfit to witness to family and friends because they remember your past.

You can always feel at ease in God's presence and enjoy your relationship with Him without guilt or shame. God is proud of you. When you came to God, He washed away your sinful past, called you His child, and gave you access to His presence at any time. You are always welcome. Your past no longer exists. God desires for you to see the brightness of His face and the wonderful future He plans for you.

God does not want you looking back and remembering your old ways. He does not think about them, and neither should you. You are a new creation in Christ Jesus.

LET GO! THE OLD LIFE IS GONE AND YOUR NEW LIFE HAS BEGUN.

YOUR SECRET PLACE

He who dwells in the secret place of the Most High shall
remain stable and fixed under the shadow of the Almighty.

PSALM 91:1 AMP

Maybe as a child, you had a special place to go when you wanted to be alone. Probably, the place was not large or fancy, but you didn't care. You were free to think things through, vent pent-up frustrations, nurse your wounds, and recoup. After spending time there, you felt better.

Now your Heavenly Father desires to be your secret place. God welcomes you to talk to Him anytime, about anything. Nothing surprises God, and He will not condemn you. Stay as long as you like and receive what you need.

God understands those special times when you just want to be quiet and bask in His love, peace, and protection. Then you can say as David did, "You will fill me with joy in Your presence" (Psalm 16:11 NIV).

GOD DELIGHTS TO FELLOWSHIP WITH YOU AND
MAKE HIS PRESENCE KNOWN, EVEN WHEN ALL YOU
WANT IS BLESSED QUIET.

RUN FOR COVER!

He will cover you with his feathers, and under his wings you will find refuge.

PSALM 91:4 NIV

Are you troubled because of the evil threats and the disastrous things happening in the world— particularly, in America? Are you afraid to be alone? Are you constantly looking over your shoulder? You are a child of God, and He loves you. God desires for you to be at peace regardless of what is happening in the world, this nation, or your own backyard. God is your provider and protector. He does not want you to be afraid or to worry about anything.

When you feel that panic is about to choke you or that fear is closing in on you, run for cover! God's covering completely surrounds and shields you. His angels encamp around you and your family. There is a special place God has planned for your safety; and His angels will lead you there to assist you and keep you from harm.

Your Heavenly Father never sleeps. God always watches over you and rejoices when you trust Him with your life.

GOD'S PROTECTION IS BETTER THAN AN INSURANCE POLICY. HE WILL KEEP YOU SAFE FROM EVERY THREAT.

KNOW YOUR RIGHTS

Woe to those who make unjust laws, to those who issue oppressive decrees, to deprive the poor of their rights and withhold justice from the oppressed of my people.

ISAIAH 10:1-2 NIV

The government makes laws and empowers certain people to enforce them. These laws state what is and is not permissible—your rights and freedom. The law helps to eliminate confusion, establish order, and provide protection. Knowing your rights as an American citizen prompts you to boldly declare what is yours and to take legal steps when those rights are violated.

When you accept Jesus as your Savior you also become a citizen in God's Kingdom (Colossians 1:13). God's Word declares your citizenship and your God-given rights. When your rights are violated, or when you have been mistreated in any way, you don't have to take matters into your own hands. Instead, run to the One who is your Advocate—the Almighty One. Trust Him to plead your case, defend your cause, and enforce your rights. God has not lost a case yet!

———

KNOW YOUR RIGHTS AND GO TO THE ONE WHO
HOLDS A HEAVENLY COURT ON YOUR BEHALF.
GOD IS ON YOUR SIDE.

YOUR FATHER'S VOICE

My sheep recognize my voice;
I know them, and they follow me.

JOHN 10:27 NLT

Parents and children have an extraordinary ability to recognize each other's voice. Even in a room filled with children, a parent knows his child's squeal of delight or cry for help. Likewise, a child athlete distinguishes his parent's cheer from the other noisy fans in the stands.

In the same way, your Heavenly Father knows your voice. He enjoys talking with you, hearing your ideas, and listening to your laugh. When you are in trouble and cry out for help, God immediately comes to your rescue. God desires for you to recognize His voice when He whispers, "Well done!" or "You didn't handle that right. Let's talk about it."

God's teaching and discipline come from His great love for you and His desire for your welfare. With God's continual assurance of love, you do not have to dread His voice. You can be at peace and say, "Yes, Father, I hear You." You can approach God's throne knowing that whatever He says is for your good. Feel free to go to God; He knows what you need to hear.

MANY VOICES CRY FOR YOUR ATTENTION, BUT ONLY THE FATHER'S VOICE BRINGS SUCCESS.

OUT OF THE BOX!

Don't become so well-adjusted to your culture that you fit into it without even thinking. Instead, fix your attention on God. You'll be changed from the inside out.

ROMANS 12:2MSG

Are you in the rut of trying to look like, talk like, and live like the Jones'? Somewhere deep inside are you crying to be set free to enjoy life?

When you are tempted to feel that no one would notice or care if you dropped off the face of the earth, go to God for assurance of His love for you. Look into God's face, and you will see how special you are to Him. In you, God created a wonderfully unique individual—there is not another like you anywhere.

God planned and created you for His pleasure and special purpose. You can measure your value by Jesus' willingness to die for you. The Master Planner and Creator joyfully waits to show you how to be the best you can be and how to live a joyful, fulfilled life. Following God's specific plan for your life blesses you—and those around you.

EACH SNOWFLAKE IS UNIQUE AND ESSENTIAL TO THE BEAUTY OF THE WHOLE. LIKEWISE, YOUR LIFE IS DIFFERENT FROM OTHERS, BUT ESSENTIAL TO ACCOMPLISHING GOD'S WILL ON EARTH.

SURE-FOOTED

He drew me up out of a horrible pit [a pit of tumult and of destruction], out of the miry clay (froth and slime), and set my feet upon a rock, steadying my steps and establishing my goings.

PSALM 40:2 AMP

You do not want to miss any God-given opportunity; but perhaps you remember a past failure, and you fear it might happen again. However, past failures do not make you a failure. God does not want you to be embarrassed or afraid to try again. Your Heavenly Father desires for you to invite Him into every part of your life. Ask God to show you His plans. God's path leads to success and victory.

God will gladly take your hand, help you find the right path, and guide you through life's decisions. And if you stumble, God is there to hold you up because He will not leave or forsake you (Deuteronomy 31:6).

FOLLOWING IN GOD'S FOOTSTEPS ASSURES
YOUR VICTORY!

COMFORT ME

You, O LORD, have helped me and comforted me.

PSALM 86:17 NIV

When you hurt as a child, maybe you climbed into your mother's lap or ran to your father's arms. In the midst of the pain, their soothing voice and close embrace made you feel that everything would be alright. Even as an adult there are times we experience pain and hurt. God wants you to find comfort in Him.

When faced with physical pain or emotional wounds, go to the One who is familiar with suffering. Jesus experienced pain; He understands. The Lord hears your cry. The Lord is ready to hold you close and dry the tears while you heal. He knows your frailties and makes His grace available to help, comfort, and heal you.

THE LORD IS FILLED WITH COMPASSION AND STANDS READY TO APPLY HIS HEALING BALM.

SOMEONE TO TALK TO

I will answer them before they even call to me.
While they are still talking to me about their needs, I will go
ahead and answer their prayers!

ISAIAH 65:24 NLT

Do you want to share some good news? Do you need a shoulder to cry on or some good advice? If so, you want to talk to a good listener. Fortunately, there is someone who is always interested in what you have to say.

You are welcome to call on God anytime because you have a direct line to His heart and immediate access to His throne. He is an excellent conversationalist. God is always ready to give you His undivided attention and patiently listen while you share your heart. You can trust God to say the right thing because He knows exactly what you need.

So, give Him a call or come visit. There is no rush—God is waiting for you.

<hr>

THERE IS ALWAYS ROOM FOR YOU NEAR
GOD'S THRONE. HIS LINES OF COMMUNICATION
ARE NEVER TOO BUSY.

BEST FRIEND

Greater love has no one than this, that he lay down his life for his friends.

JOHN 15:13 NIV

Is there someone who is so near to your heart that you consider him or her your best friend? Maybe it is hard to find the right words to describe just how much this person means to you.

Jesus, your Lord and Savior, would like to be your best friend? Will you let Jesus be your constant, faithful companion—the one who is closely involved with every part of your life?

Jesus can go with you everywhere. Jesus is generous and kind; He is willing to help you anytime you need Him. He is a trustworthy confidant and wise counselor who will tell you the truth without condemning or ridiculing you.

You can be at ease in the Lord's presence because He understands and accepts you. The Lord has great plans for your future. He anticipates your success and wants to participate. Jesus knows you better and loves you more than anyone else. You could not ask for a better best friend. Jesus called His disciples His friends. He taught them and ministered alongside them. Jesus is your Friend, too.

YOU CAN TRUST JESUS WITH YOUR LIFE BECAUSE HE GAVE HIS LIFE FOR YOU.

TAKE YOUR STAND!

And he will stand, for the Lord is able to make him stand.

ROMANS 14:4 NIV

Have you prayed about something for a long time and not received an answer or seen a change? Maybe you have been standing in faith so long that you feel like your spiritual legs are shaking and your knees are about to buckle.

Do not lose heart! God promises to hear and answer your prayers. Your job is to hold firm to that promise and to continue praying and believing. God will strengthen your heart and make you steady as He firmly sets your feet on the rock of Jesus Christ (1 Corinthians 10:4). Then the storms of life will not cause you to fall.

When you are satisfied that you have done all that God has said, stand strong knowing that He will be faithful to His word.

NO MATTER WHAT YOU ARE FACING, YOU CAN BE SURE OF THIS—GOD'S PLAN WILL STAND STRONG.

A LOVE LIKE NO OTHER

See how very much our heavenly Father loves us, for he allows us to be called his children.

1 JOHN 3:1 NLT

Even though you know family and friends love you, there are times you want to hear them say it. A sincere "I love you" warms and reassures the listener.

Your Heavenly Father does not hesitate to let you know how much He loves you. God's love for you is everlasting and boundless because God loves you as much as He loves Christ Jesus. God's unconditional love goes far beyond human reason and understanding. The supernatural power of God's love speaks to the deepest needs within your heart.

No other voice is as sweet as the Lord's when He says, "I love you." God's voice erases all doubts. As you nestle in God's arms, listen closely while He rejoices over you with singing.

———

IF NO ONE HAS SAID "I LOVE YOU" TODAY, THEN LET GOD BE THE FIRST. HE WILL SAY IT WITH JOY.

PATIENCE, PLEASE!

For you have need of steadfast patience and endurance,
so that you may perform and fully accomplish the will of God,
and thus receive and carry away [and enjoy to the full]
what is promised.

HEBREWS 10:36 AMP

With technology has come the ability to get things done fast. In fact, technology streamlines our lives so well that we forget how to wait. Although learning patience is difficult, the quality of patience produces happiness, peace, and success.

If you are disappointed or frustrated by life in spite of your best efforts, then God will help you patiently stay on course while He takes care of things for you. God will empower you to exercise patience when you, or others, make mistakes. Not only will God help you get up and try again when you fall, but He will also teach you how to wait for Him to answer your prayers. Trust God to take you to victory—one step at a time.

PATIENCE EQUIPS YOU TO REMAIN STABLE AS YOU
TRUST GOD TO TEACH YOU TO HANDLE LIFE'S UPS
AND DOWNS.

INTO HIS MARVELOUS LIGHT

*For you are all children of the light and of the day;
we don't belong to darkness and night.*

1 THESSALONIANS 5:5 NLT

Are you feeling alone, insecure, and vulnerable? Then refuse to allow darkness to press in on you. You can escape. Your Heavenly Father faithfully keeps His promises, and He will never leave you.

Even in the darkness, the Lord brings light to your life. And light overcomes the darkness every time! Like a floodlight on a dark path, you can see clearly when you walk in the light of His presence. Step by step, His Word is the lamp for your feet and the light for your path (Psalm 119:105). Though darkness surrounds you, arise because God's glory shines upon you and makes you a light in the world to show others the way.

IN HIS PRESENCE, YOUR FUTURE IS ALWAYS BRIGHT.

YOUR JOB—AND GOD'S JOB

Do not let your hearts be troubled and do not be afraid.
JOHN 14:27 NIV

Over one hundred years ago, Hannah Whitall Smith wrote what has become a Christian classic, *The Christian's Secret of a Happy Life.* One chapter is titled "Man's Job" and another chapter "God's Job." Her point? Your job is to trust God, and His job is to take care of you. That is just as true for personal peace as it is for any other need.

But what does that mean practically? It means that you push away the lies you hear in your head that tell you that God will not help you, that God is not really good, or that you are disqualified because Christ's sacrifice does not cover your particular failings. Refuse to believe these lies and replace them with God's promises of faithfulness, forgiveness, love, and peace. Philippians 4:6-7 says that if you tell God your problems and thank Him for your blessings, then His peace will guard your heart.

SO WHO ARE YOU GOING TO BELIEVE? THE LIES? OR GOD? MAKE A DECISION NOT TO ENTERTAIN THE LIES, AND GOD PROMISES TO DO THE REST.

JUST ASK!

If you remain in me and my words remain in you, ask whatever you wish, and it will be given you.

JOHN 15:7 NIV

As a child, you probably felt more comfortable asking your parents for something you needed rather than for something you wanted. For instance, asking for shoes instead of a bicycle. Probably they would buy the needed shoes right away, but they would wait for a special occasion to buy the bicycle—like your birthday or Christmas.

Perhaps you feel the same way in your relationship with God. You are comfortable asking God for the raise that you need so desperately; however, a new car is too much to ask for if the one you have runs well.

Nevertheless, your Heavenly Father wants you to be as comfortable asking for your desires as you are asking Him to supply your needs. Don't hesitate to ask Him. If you delight in doing what God wants, then He delights in giving you your heart's desire (Psalm 37:4).

❧

IN ALL THINGS, GOD WANTS YOU TO ASK ACCORDING TO HIS WILL AND BELIEVE THAT HE GIVES GENEROUSLY TO HIS CHILDREN.

HE HAS MADE ME GLAD!

This is the day which the Lord has brought about;
we will rejoice and be glad in it.

PSALM 118:24 AMP

When your attitude turns sour, ask God to help you control it. Allow God to transform your negative attitude into a sweet, refreshing victory. God created your emotions, and He will teach you to keep them balanced and controlled. God understands—He is touched by your feelings (Hebrews 4:15).

Think on God's Word, character, and nature. Focus on spiritual things rather than circumstances around you. As you think on these things, your mind and emotions become stable.

WITH HIS HELP YOU CAN STEP OFF THE EMOTIONAL ROLLER COASTER AND REST IN THE PEACE OF GOD.

TRYING TO PLEASE

For they loved the approval and the praise and the glory that come from men [instead of and] more than the glory that comes from God. [They valued their credit with men more than their credit with God.]

JOHN 12:43 AMP

Sometimes it seems difficult to please people, no matter how hard you try. However, you cannot become so concerned with pleasing people that you allow feelings of rejection, inferiority, and low self-esteem to creep in.

God knows that you are sincere, and He is pleased that you desire to obey Him and bless others. Ask God to teach you how to prioritize and keep a healthy balance in all you do and in all your relationships—beginning with Him. You are God's creation, adopted as His child, and crowned with His dignity. Your worth and value come from Him.

When your best is not good enough for others, remember that God loves you for who you are— not what you do.

———

WHEN IT SEEMS THAT YOU CAN'T PLEASE OTHERS— PUT A SMILE ON GOD'S FACE AND YOURS BY DOING WHAT GOD DESIRES!

SAY IT RIGHT

*Listen, for I have worthy things to say; I open my lips
to speak what is right. My mouth speaks what is true,
for my lips detest wickedness.*

PROVERBS 8:6-7 NIV

Have you ever said something that you regret?
Perhaps later, your regret affects your communication with God. *Me and my big mouth! I
shouldn't have said that! Why do I always say the
wrong thing?* Or *Why didn't I speak up and say
something?*

When you have God's Word planted deep
within your heart, you can pray and talk with
others effectively. The Holy Spirit helps you; He
helps you think before you speak and reminds you
of what God's Word says.

Then you will speak the words of truth,
wisdom, love, faith, peace, joy, and victory that
please God, encourage yourself, and bless others.
Your tongue will be like the pen of a skillful writer
confidently declaring, "This is what the Lord
says." You will rest knowing that God carries out
His Word.

THE ART OF GOOD CONVERSATION BENEFITS
EVERYONE.

STAY COOL!

My dear brothers, take note of this: Everyone should be quick to listen, slow to speak and slow to become angry, for man's anger does not bring about the righteous life that God desires.

JAMES 1:19-20 NIV

It is hard to keep from getting angry when someone mistreats you or hurts your feelings. More than likely, your first response is, "Who do you think you are? How dare you!" You probably feel that you must defend your dignity. But after a cooling off period, you wonder if you could have handled the situation in a better way.

The fight-or-flight response causes you to use whatever is necessary to defend yourself—whether it be physical blows or emotional, verbal outbursts. Only God can help you control the impulse to retaliate. Put your wounded feelings and your anger in God's hands, and trust Him to take care of the situation. Then you can rejoice in victory without any regrets.

SITTING DOWN WITH GOD SOOTHES ANGER LIKE WATER ON A FLAME. AFTER A FEW MINUTES WITH HIM, YOU ARE READY TO RESPOND WITH HIS CHARACTER AND NATURE.

YOUR ADVANTAGE

I pray that God will take care of all your needs with the
wonderful blessings that come from Christ Jesus!

PHILIPPIANS 4:19 CEV

Are you wondering what your purpose is or what your future has in store? If so, you are not alone. Even the people who seem to have it all together have questions and feel uncertain about their lives. Fortunately, you have an advantage over many people—you know exactly who to go to for your answers.

Long before He made the world, God chose you to be His child. In His love and wisdom, He already made plans and prepared a path for you. He watches over you and patiently teaches you; but, you have the freedom to make your own decisions. Should you take a wrong turn, He will help you get back on course. God will steady your faltering steps, guide you through unfamiliar territory, straighten crooked paths, and lead you safely around traps.

God will take care of you so that you can accomplish His purposes in your life.

———

YOUR HEAVENLY FATHER PLANS FOR EACH STEP AND
EVERY DAY OF YOUR LIFE TO BE A SUCCESS.

AGAINST ALL ODDS

Be brave and confident! There's no reason to be afraid . . . We are much more powerful, because the LORD our God fights on our side.

2 CHRONICLES 32:7-8 CEV

When you stand for truth, seen and unseen forces will confront and oppose you.

If you are beginning to feel like the victim instead of the victor, then take heart because Almighty God is with you. He—the Lord of hosts, "God of the Angel Armies" (Isaiah 19:4 MSG)—surrounds you. God's presence in you is far stronger than anything in the world, and He is more powerful than the forces opposing you.

Accept God's invitation to boldly come to His throne and ask for His help when you need it. You become courageous and strong in God's mighty power when you believe His promises. God promises that your enemy will run from you, and not one of God's promises will fail.

THE MAKER OF HEAVEN AND EARTH IS IN YOU, WITH YOU, FOR YOU, AROUND YOU, AND ON YOUR SIDE. THEREFORE, YOUR SUCCESS IS GUARANTEED.

BY MY SIDE

I'll be with you. I won't give up on you; I won't leave you.

JOSHUA 1:5 MSG

Have you ever felt alone even though you were in a crowd? Feeling lonely can result from the death of a spouse, the breakup of a close relationship, moving to a new neighborhood, or not having a date. You might be tempted to curl up into a protective shell and withdraw from others. You think, *If only I had someone with me my loneliness would end.*

However, someone is with you; and He is the greatest companion you can ever have. God stands by your side to make you whole, strong, and sufficient in Him.

Mother Teresa of Calcutta once said, "Loneliness and the feeling of being unwanted is the most terrible poverty." As you thank God for your loyal friends and companions, never forget the One who enriches your life as no other can.

WITH GOD YOU ARE THE MAJORITY INSTEAD OF THE MINORITY.

WITHOUT FAIL

*Know in all your hearts and in all your souls that not one thing
has failed of all the good things which the Lord your God
promised concerning you. All have come to pass for you;
not one thing of them has failed.*

JOSHUA 23:14 AMP

What a wonderful world it would be if no one ever made a mistake. However, God's perfection is unattainable for us. That is why our Heavenly Father sent His Son. Jesus never disobeyed; yet He died for you. The Lord graciously forgives all your shortcomings and failures.

When others fail you, ask God to help you forgive them just as He has forgiven you. Because under the right circumstances, even a trustworthy person with sincere intentions will fall short.

God's Word is true—it is impossible for Him to lie. God will do what He promises, and He will never betray you.

GOD HAS GIVEN YOU HIS WORD—
AND HIS WORD NEVER FAILS.

THE RIGHTFUL OWNER

Then he assigned an official to her case and said to him, "Give back everything that belonged to her, including all the income from her land from the day she left the country until now."

2 KINGS 8:6 NIV

Your possessions result from your labor or gifts from other people. Furthermore, your possessions rightfully belong to you; therefore, you protect them from theft or harm.

God also gives you heavenly gifts: love, peace, joy, health, and success. God desires for you to use and enjoy His gifts. Sometimes, however, life's pressures can cause you to be careless with God's blessings.

Ask God to help you be as mindful and responsible for His invisible blessings as you are with your material possessions. God will show you what caused your temporary setback and help you recover your heavenly gifts.

———

EVEN MORE GIVING THAN AN EARTHLY FATHER,
GOD SHOWERS YOU WITH GOOD GIFTS.

THE BEST DEFENSE

No weapon that is formed against you shall prosper, and every tongue that shall rise against you in judgment you shall show to be in the wrong. This [peace, righteousness, security, triumph over opposition] is the heritage of the servants of the Lord.

ISAIAH 54:17 AMP

The insult and humiliation of being wrongfully accused of something is almost unbearable. You may even think you have the right to defend yourself. After all, if you do not defend yourself, then who will?

The Lord is the Wonderful Counselor who carries the government upon His shoulders, and He is also the righteous judge who defends you. Nothing is hidden from Him. God will expose the false accusations against you. God lights your path because you are truthful and innocent, but those who plot and lie will stumble in darkness and fall into the traps they set for you.

Do not fear or be intimidated by your accusers. Instead, choose to rejoice, stand firm, and hold onto your peace as God fights your battle. The truth will prove your innocence. God on your side is the best defense.

GOD'S CLOSING ARGUMENTS ON YOUR BEHALF CANNOT BE DISPUTED, AND HIS JUSTICE IS INFALLIBLE.

TRUSTWORTHY

When I am afraid, I put my trust in you.
PSALM 56:3 NRSV

Your children have made bad decisions. You wonder, How can they be so blind? How will they repair the damage? Who can reach them? You let your mind imagine the worst. It is time to try something new: trust God for the outcome. You must believe that God loves you, and your children, and focus on His love.

Instead of rehearsing all the bad things that could happen, remind yourself of God's faithfulness. Philippians 4:8 KJV says, "Finally, brethren, whatsoever things are true, whatsoever things are honest, whatsoever things are just, whatsoever things are pure, whatsoever things are lovely, whatsoever things are of good report; if there be any virtue, and if there be any praise, think on these things."

When you read your Bible and spend time with God, you will discover He is in control of the circumstances that terrify you. He promises to be faithful. When you are tempted to fear, think about His love. He will never leave you or your children. God's love for you makes Him worthy of your trust.

BUILD YOUR TRUST IN GOD BY READING OF
HIS LOVE FOR YOU IN THE BIBLE.

DIVINE BENEFITS

*Praise the LORD, O my soul and forget not all his benefits—
who forgives all your sins and heals all your diseases,
who redeems your life from the pit and crowns you with love
and compassion, who satisfies your desires with good things so
that your youth is renewed like the eagle's.*

PSALM 103:2-5 NIV

You appreciate the benefits that make life more enjoyable. Consider how a good benefits package on your job affects your life. Even if the work is demanding, your attitude and commitment improve when you know that your employer provides for your needs.

Every good and perfect gift comes from God, and He has promised not to withhold any good thing from you. When life's disappointments and troubles sour your outlook, concentrate on God's promises. If you allow God to tell you about the benefits that He provides (Psalm 68:19 KJV), then you will rejoice because He makes your life worth living.

YOU ARE THE BENEFICIARY OF GOD'S GOODNESS.

No Ego Trip

*First pride, then the crash—the bigger the ego,
the harder the fall.*

PROVERBS 16:18 MSG

Jesus desired for people to see God's love, grace, mercy, and power in all that He did. Jesus did not try to make himself famous, but gave God all the praise for the wonderful miracles that happened.

If you find yourself desiring recognition and applause, then pray instead for the humility to give thanks to God. The Lord is the One who is truly good, and every good thing comes from Him. Humility acknowledges that you live in God and that you can do nothing without Him.

You are a vessel that manifests God's goodness. When someone compliments you, thank them sincerely. But more importantly, remember to thank your Heavenly Father.

It's easy to wear humility when you meditate on God's goodness to you.

THERE IS HOPE

*Remember [fervently] the word and promise to Your servant,
in which You have caused me to hope.*

PSALM 119:49 AMP

Many people experience a plateau in which it appears that their faith is at a standstill and their hope is almost gone. In those moments, weariness and hopelessness can cloud the mind and try to block God's victory.

For you, the hardest part of the struggle might be continuing to hope in God's Word. However, be confident that you will receive what God has promised and keep rejoicing in your hope.

Do not give up—God's Word will not fail you. Hold fast to His Word because it has the power to change any circumstance. God will strengthen your trust in Him so that you can hold on. Not only will God keep your hope alive, but He will also provide a solution to the problem. The Lord is your hope, and He will make you glad that you did not give up.

THERE IS NOTHING TOO HARD FOR GOD.

STIRRED UP!

I would remind you to stir up (rekindle the embers of, fan the flame of, and keep burning) the [gracious] gift of God, [the inner fire] that is in you.

2 TIMOTHY 1:6 AMP

Your salvation opens doors to a new life and a new excitement in God. It is important to keep your excitement fueled with fervor for God's Word, His truth, and His love for you.

Thank God for the wonderful things that He has done for you. You are a new creation in Him, and you think in new ways. God puts a new spirit within you and gives you His power to live a new life. God gives you a new name and even a new song to sing—something even the angels do not have.

Let an attitude of thankfulness stir up a new zeal about God's goodness and all His plans for you. Then each day will be a new beginning.

YOUR HEAVENLY FATHER DESIRES THAT YOU ENJOY LIFE. AS YOU CLOSELY FOLLOW HIM, EXPECTANTLY WATCH FOR THE HEAVENLY TREASURES AWAITING YOU.

POWER TO RESIST

No test or temptation that comes your way is beyond the course of what others have had to face. All you need to remember is that God will never let you down; he'll never let you be pushed past your limit; he'll always be there to help you come through it.

1 CORINTHIANS 10:13 MSG

Christianity does not exempt you from normal thoughts and feelings. Although you are capable of experiencing temptation, your Heavenly Father's presence is greater than the temptation. God gives you His power, and you can resist temptation.

In His infinite wisdom and understanding, God gives you the Holy Spirit to help control human impulses and resist temptation. God also gives you His Word to show you what is right. Your resistance to temptation proves that you are maturing in godliness.

WHEN TEMPTATIONS COME, TURN YOUR THOUGHTS TOWARD GOD'S POWER AND HIS ABILITY TO OVERCOME THEM IN YOU.

FORGIVEN

*He is so rich in kindness that he purchased our freedom
through the blood of his Son, and our sins are forgiven.*

EPHESIANS 1:7 NLT

You admit your mistake and ask for forgiveness, but perhaps you find yourself still
mentally rehearsing it. You beat yourself up
emotionally; and your inability to forgive yourself
interrupts your sleep, hinders your job performance, and separates you from loved ones. Worst of
all, a lack of forgiveness can even cause you to pull
away from God.

Let go! Your Heavenly Father forgives you
when you confess the mistake, and He promises
not to think of it again. In spite of your guilt,
accept God's forgiveness by forgiving yourself.
God has the last word; so, instead of remembering
your sin, surrender to His love. God desires to fill
your life with His goodness. Come like a small
child and rest in your Father's arms.

———

GOD'S LOVE MOTIVATES HIM TO FORGIVE YOU.
YOUR LOVE FOR GOD SHOULD MOTIVATE YOU TO
FORGIVE YOURSELF.

THE REAL REASON

*I searched everywhere, determined to find wisdom and to
understand the reason for things.*

ECCLESIASTES 7:25 NLT

There is a reason for everything you say and do.
God desires for you to be truthful in every
way, beginning with your motives. When your
motives are right, your attitude and behavior will
be right. Were you ever troubled because you
started to do something that seemed right at first,
but later felt wrong? Why the sudden change?
Perhaps when it first crossed your mind you
thought of several convincing justifications for
your actions, but now you have doubts. Search
your heart and ask yourself, What is my real
reason for doing this?

A sincere heart pleases God. Come to Him and
discuss your plans. God's Word will judge your
deepest thoughts and motives. God's Word
prepares you to be honest with God, with yourself,
and with others. Consequently, your motives and
actions will please God.

TIME IN GOD'S PRESENCE ALLOWS YOU TO
EXPERIENCE GOD'S HEART AND PROVIDES WISDOM
FOR A GODLY LIFE!

SAVED FROM DISTRESS

"LORD, help!" they cried in their trouble, and he saved them from their distress.

PSALM 107:13 NLT

Do you feel overwhelmed today? You might feel yourself sinking as troubling waters swirl about you, and you are convinced that your situation will not improve. Even now, God is your help. Even now, His mighty arm can reach down and save you.

You may not be able to control your circumstances, but God can. And you are in control of your response to the situation. Take your eyes off the debt, destruction, confusion, and grief—and look to your heavenly Father. He will lift you up. God will make a way where there seems to be no way. Most likely, God will find a solution that you have not considered. It may even appear to be a more difficult path, but follow Him anyway. God will lead you out of your distress along the best path.

Are you ready to give up? Don't! God loves you and hears your cry for help. You might not see the answer the moment you ask for help, but He won't let you down. Hold tightly to God's promise never to leave you. He loves you with an everlasting love.

GOD HAS THE ANSWER FOR EVERY DISTRESS.

BELIEVE IT!

It's impossible to please God apart from faith. And why?
Because anyone who wants to approach God must believe both
that he exists and that he cares enough to respond to those
who seek him.

HEBREWS 11:6 MSG

You are facing what appears to be the toughest situation you have ever dealt with. You continually wrestle with the problem and seek an answer to the recurring question: How am I going to get out of this mess? In despair, you finally admit that the problem is too much for you to handle. You are no closer to solving the problem than you were when it first happened. And your efforts to fix it without God's help have made it worse.

In desperation you cry out to God, but your faith seems so small for such a large problem. Besides, why should He answer now when I should have prayed from the start? And why should He help now when I tried to handle it all by myself?

God honors faith—however small. You must believe that He loves and cares for you. God is on your side, and He is greater than your problem. If you are wrong, then pray, Lord, forgive me and help me. God hears you, and help is on the way. As you walk with Him daily, use every experience to increase your faith in God's ability to care for you.

GOD PROMISES THAT HIS WORD WILL DO
WHAT IT SAYS. YOU CAN BELIEVE HIM
ABOVE ALL ELSE.

THE EMPTY NEST

He gives childless couples a family, gives them joy as the parents of children. Hallelujah!

PSALM 113:9 MSG

You do not understand why you and your spouse are having such a hard time trying to have children. Unwanted and abused children confuse and grieve you. You both want a big family. Right after you married, the two of you began making plans so that everything would be ready when you started your family. But, the children never arrived.

Your Heavenly Father feels your anguish and sees your tears. God purposes for husbands and wives to enjoy bearing and raising children. God told Adam and Eve to be fruitful and multiply. Like you, God also desires to have children. You are one of them. You are precious to God, and He desires for you to cast all your hurt and hopelessness on Him. God will help you believe His promises. In the Old Testament, Sarah and Hannah were childless, but God blessed them with children. God will be faithful to you, too.

———

WAIT ON GOD AND ALLOW HIM TO SOLVE
YOUR PROBLEMS. OUR WONDERFUL GOD TURNS THE
IMPOSSIBLE INTO THE POSSIBLE WHEN
YOU TRUST HIM.

WHICH WAY, LORD?

You said to me, "I will point out the road that you should follow. I will be your teacher and watch over you."

PSALM 32:8 CEV

Even in the midst of your busy life, you can know which way to go. Before your Heavenly Father created the universe, He planned and established His divine order. God is not confused or chaotic, and He does not desire for your life to be chaotic either.

God goes before you and straightens the crooked paths. The Lord is the leader; and when you choose to follow Him, the road before you is clear. As His child, feel free to ask God to show you the path to walk so that you become wise, strong, and confident in Him. God knows what is best for you. In His presence you will escape from turmoil and find peace.

───

WHEN PLANNING A TRIP, YOU USE A ROAD MAP. SOMETIMES THE MAP SHOWS SEVERAL WAYS TO REACH YOUR DESTINATION. LIFE ALSO HAS DIFFERENT PATHS TO FOLLOW. TRUST GOD TO LEAD YOU ALONG THE RIGHT PATH.

DEBT OF LOVE

Pay all your debts, except the debt of love for others. You can never finish paying that!

ROMANS 13:8 NLT

*D*ear Lord, how do You manage to love and forgive multitudes of unkind people when I am having such a hard time forgiving these few?

It seems you whispered that question a hundred times today. Someone was unkind to you from the moment you stepped outside your front door until you arrived home. The entire day you prayed for those who offended you. You asked God to strengthen your love so that you could forgive them. Forgiveness was difficult each time, but His grace empowered you to persevere.

The day has come to an end, and now you bask in your heavenly Father's love. He soothes your hurt feelings and washes away the remembrance of today's offenses. You think of the love that caused Jesus to die for you, and your heart swells with gratitude. You are so indebted to Him. How can you repay Jesus? Then the Holy Spirit reminds you of your prayers, love, and forgiveness toward others today. As you enjoy His presence, allow His strength to equip you for tomorrow because love's debt never ends.

THE ONLY DEBT GOD APPROVES OF IS LOVE. LOVE CAN NEVER BE PAID OFF, BUT GOD HELPS YOU PAY SOMETHING ON IT EVERY DAY.

FAVORITE CHILD

Do not want anything that belongs to someone else. Don't want anyone's house, wife or husband, slaves, oxen, donkeys or anything else.

EXODUS 20:17 CEV

Have you ever listened to a speaker who made you feel like you were the only one in the room, yet the room was full of people? You are God's favorite child. Even with a world full of people, He is focused on you. You never have to feel left out when others receive a blessing.

God wants you to be convinced of His love and know that He does not favor someone more than you. Ask Him to help you put others' concerns before your own. Let His Spirit stir up sincere joy in you when others are blessed. As you continue to obey Him, a time will come when others will rejoice with you. Expect it to happen sooner than you think!

❧

YOUR FATHER REJOICES OVER YOU—
HIS FAVORITE CHILD!

A ROLE MODEL

*Pattern yourselves after me [follow my example], as I imitate
and follow Christ (the Messiah).*

1 CORINTHIANS 11:1 AMP

Lately, you have been disturbed about your
child's behavior. You are hurt and disappointed
because your children deliberately disobey you.
But you are more disappointed with yourself
because you feel that you have not been a good
example for your children to follow. *Dear Lord, I
feel like I have failed You and my children! Where
did I go wrong?*

God has not forgotten that you trained your
children in His Word. God remembers your
prayers asking for help in modeling godly
behavior. Your godly instruction is firmly rooted in
your children's hearts. The Holy Spirit will bring
instruction to your children's mind at the
appropriate time. Regardless of your children's
mistakes, God's compassionate heart will forgive
them. God's grace and mercy continually hover
over your children to keep them safe.

Your children will not forget how you love
and obey God. The Lord loves your children as
much as He loves you. Because of your godly
example, your children will also love and follow
God.

ALLOW YOUR CHILDREN TO WATCH AS YOU FOLLOW
CHRIST. YOUR GODLY WORDS AND ACTIONS TEACH
THEM TO LOVE AND OBEY GOD.

A FAMILY AFFAIR

As for me and my family, we'll worship GOD.
JOSHUA 24:15 MSG

Diligent worship, prayer, and study of God's Word bring tremendous growth. Your life today is vastly different than your life before God. But unfortunately, your relatives and friends are not enthusiastic about your new life. They avoid you, make sarcastic remarks, and joke about something that is dear to you. Although they often hurt you, you tell them of God's love without pressuring them. Why can't they see the wonderful change in your life? *Lord, I thought that my life would encourage them to seek You, but it seems that the opposite has happened. Please help me reach them.*

Your love and concern come from God's compassionate heart. God desires for your loved ones to come to Him even more than you do. God wants your friends and family to receive His love and the new life He has for them. Believe and pray that they will want to know the loving God who made such a wonderful change in you. You have done what God asked, and He does not want you to be discouraged and disappointed.

—⚬⚬⚬—

AS YOU CONTINUE TO LOVE AND PRAY FOR YOUR
LOVED ONES, TRUST GOD TO DO THE REST.

A JOB WELL DONE

Make it your ambition to lead a quiet life, to mind your own business and to work with your hands, just as we told you, so that your daily life may win the respect of outsiders and so that you will not be dependent on anybody.

1 THESSALONIANS 4:11-12 NIV

For years you have been a dependable, productive, and valuable employee. You receive great job appraisals. But today, the company let you go due to downsizing.

Dear God, this is the only kind of work I know. How am I going to provide for my family? I just can't start all over again! Please show me what to do and help my family!

Before your plea escapes your lips, God has plans to help your family through this tough time. Stay in God's presence and allow His love and peace to remove the feelings of anger, self-pity, and fear. Remind yourself of God's faithfulness and goodness. God carried you through the difficulties the last time. As you meditate on God's faithfulness to you in the past, your doubt will yield to trust in Him.

GOD IS THE SOURCE OF THE WISDOM, SKILL, AND CREATIVITY YOU NEED TO SUCCESSFULLY DO YOUR JOB. SPEND TIME WITH THE SOURCE OF YOUR SUCCESS.

FOLLOW THE LEADER

Pray for all people. As you make your requests, plead for God's mercy upon them, and give thanks. Pray this way for kings and all others who are in authority, so that we can live in peace and quietness, in godliness and dignity. This is good and pleases God our Savior.

1 TIMOTHY 2:1-3 NLT

*L*ord, how can I respect and obey a leader who does not know how to lead? He doesn't know what he's doing, but I'm expected to do what he says?

Having to obey an unqualified leader is frustrating, but sometimes you have no choice. So, what can you do about it?

The answer is simple, but powerful—pray. The sweet presence of God is available to help you. Ask with humility, and the Holy Spirit will show you how to pray for your leader. God's Word says that He will change the heart of a leader to obey His will. Your prayers bring godly change.

Ask God for compassion; remember that your leader is human and imperfect—just like you. Pray that your leader will hear and obey God. And believe that God will correct your leader's mistakes. God desires for us to honor, obey, and pray for our leaders.

REJOICE KNOWING THAT GOD HAS A PURPOSE FOR YOU EVERYWHERE YOU GO. GOD'S PRESENCE IN YOU WILL HELP YOUR LEADER FULFILL GOD'S PURPOSE FOR BOTH OF YOU.

TRY, TRY AGAIN

Though a righteous man falls seven times, he rises again.

PROVERBS 24:16 NIV

Why should I keep trying when I continue to mess up? I'm tired of the whole thing, and I'm not going to embarrass myself by trying again!

Your heavenly Father knows about your efforts. He understands your weariness and disappointment. But God does not see you as a quitter. Nor is God angry with you. In fact, you are probably the only one who is giving yourself such a hard time about your failures.

Before you say something negative about yourself, go to your heavenly Father. Let God's love comfort you. Allow His peace to wash away the anxiety and frustration. Place your wounded self-image in God's hands and let Him heal it.

You can rise with hope and dignity when you believe what God's Word says about you. As you look to God for help, you can face the challenge again with renewed strength and the determination to overcome. God already sees you as the victor, but He desires that you know it for yourself.

GOD GIVES STRENGTH AND COURAGE TO SUCCEED
NO MATTER HOW LONG IT TAKES.

THE REASON FOR LIVING

None of us lives to himself [but to the Lord].

ROMANS 14:7 AMP

Life is good. Yet joy and satisfaction are short-lived, and you yearn for fulfillment. A deeper and richer meaning seems missing from your life.

Lord, I'm thankful for the good life I have, but I feel there is more than what I'm experiencing right now. Please show me what's missing.

It might be that you are seeking God's purpose for you. Yes, your love and obedience please God. However, the Lord has a specific place in the Body of Christ for you. God created you for a unique purpose. The Bible is filled with loyal believers—Abraham, Moses, Mary, David, Esther, and Paul to name a few. Just as these heroes of our faith once witnessed God's presence, experienced His goodness, and obeyed His will; so can you!

Seek God's heart. Ask God to show you His desires. Let God reveal His purpose for you and enjoy the fulfillment of walking with Him.

YOUR HEAVENLY FATHER'S PURPOSE FOR YOUR LIFE
BRINGS JOY AND FULFILLMENT.

OUT OF HARM'S WAY

Keep me safe, O God, for I have come to you for refuge. . . . I know the LORD is always with me. I will not be shaken, for he is right beside me. No wonder my heart is filled with joy, and my mouth shouts his praises! My body rests in safety.

PSALM 16:1,8-9 NLT

It is easy to become fearful when you dwell on the crime, violence, and threats of terrorism that are occuring in the world today. Although you pray and trust God, fearful thoughts creep in. Maybe you wonder if your faith is strong enough to trust in God's protection.

God gives you His Word, and He will not allow any evil thing to succeed against you. God protects His people from all threats (Deuteronomy 28:7). When you feel unsafe, run to God. The Lord builds an impenetrable wall around you, lays a covering of protection over you, and provides a strong tower to shelter you. God commands His angels to watch over you and keep you safe.

PLACE YOUR LIFE IN GOD'S HANDS,
AND THE ONE WHO GAVE HIS LIFE FOR YOU WILL
KEEP YOU SECURE.

WHY DID IT HAPPEN?

*"Do not be afraid . . . You are mine. When you go through
deep waters and great trouble, I will be with you."*

ISAIAH 43:1-2 NLT

Since the terrible accident, the days are as dark
and lonely as the nights. Between the countless
calls and visits, you try to understand, but logic
escapes you. Your heart cries, *Why, Lord?*

Your Heavenly Father understands your
emotions. Your situation seems unbearable, but
God knows what you need. You can hold on to
Him and cry for as long as necessary. You can lay
your head on God's shoulder without speaking a
word, and He will understand. Don't rush, because
God has plenty of time. Your recovery and healing
begin in God's presence.

Tragedy causes people to turn from God or
run to Him. Though your weeping may last
awhile, God promises His joy will strengthen you
to face tomorrow. (See Psalm 30:5.) But for now,
just rest in God's arms and receive His peace.

GOD'S LOVING HEART AND OUTSTRETCHED ARMS ARE
ALWAYS READY TO COMFORT YOU THROUGH
HEARTACHE AND DESPAIR.

ALL MY FAULT!

*And, beloved, if our consciences (our hearts) do not accuse us
[if they do not make us feel guilty and condemn us], we have
confidence (complete assurance and boldness) before God.*

1 JOHN 3:21 AMP

Guilt makes you wish you could punish yourself. You mistakenly think you would feel better if you did. You think, *If only I had (or had not)* . . . And an apology does not seem adequate. Once again, you prayerfully try to figure out how to correct your wrong.

Your Heavenly Father allowed Jesus to be punished for your sins. As a result, God forgives you and holds nothing against you. God's Word says you are not condemned. As His child, God forgives you when you ask. God does not bring it up again.

God knows that you are remorseful, and He hears your penitent prayer. Now God waits to lift the burden of guilt so that you can enjoy the freedom of a clear conscience and a joyful heart. God makes His grace available to help you avoid the same mistake. Put past failures behind you, and you will have fresh hope for tomorrow.

IN THE ARMS OF YOUR FATHER, THERE IS NO
CONDEMNATION. HIS LOVE, GRACE, AND MERCY ARE
GREATER THAN YOUR SIN.

THE PERFECT COVER

*Above all things have intense and unfailing love for one
another, for love covers a multitude of sins [forgives and
disregards the offenses of others].*

1 PETER 4:8 AMP

You just witnessed something that could
absolutely ruin the reputation of the person
who mistreated you. You could easily get even by
telling others what you saw and heard. *And who
could blame me? After all, I saw what they did.*
However, you know God is not pleased with spite-
fulness.

Yes, it is unfair for you to suffer for something
you did not do—even more unfair when the one
mistreating you seems to get away with doing
wrong. But the Lord is on your side; He will make
things right for you in His perfect time. You do
not need to know how, when, or where God will
deal with the problem.

Trust Him to cover you with His love and
peace while you cover the one who mistreated you
with forgiveness and prayer. Now you can rejoice
knowing that your Heavenly Father has it all
under control.

BECAUSE GOD'S LOVE AND MERCY COVER YOUR
FAULTS, IT IS NOW EASIER TO COVER SOMEONE ELSE'S
FAULTS WITH FORGIVENESS AND PRAYER.

A GOOD RETURN

Give, and [gifts] will be given to you; good measure, pressed down, shaken together, and running over. . . . For with the measure you deal out [with the measure you use when you confer benefits on others], it will be measured back to you.

LUKE 6:38 AMP

You are facing a large bill that has to be paid today, and there is not enough money in your account. You handle your money wisely, pay your bills on time, and honor God by obeying Him with your money. You pray, but time is running out; and the money still has not shown up.

Your Heavenly Father does not forget your obedience or your willingness to help others. Your honesty and integrity please the Lord. God keeps His word. The Lord promises to be with you in trouble and to deliver you. God will help you because you help others.

The Lord never disappoints you. The Holy Spirit empowers you to apply the pressure of faith in God's Word against the financial pressure. Now you can look to God with a thankful heart and expect your financial help to come right on time!

GIVING WITH A RIGHT HEART CAUSES YOUR GIFT TO BE MEASURED BACK TO YOU.

UNASHAMED

For I am not ashamed of the Gospel (good news) of Christ, for it is God's power working unto salvation [for deliverance from eternal death] to everyone who believes with a personal trust and a confident surrender and firm reliance.

ROMANS 1:16 AMP

Do you remember the joy and excitement you felt when you first fell in love with Jesus? You felt so free and wished everyone could feel the same way. You disliked anything that resembled wrongdoing, and you were not embarrassed to stand for right.

Perhaps now, you are quiet and reserved—almost timid about your walk with God. Relatives, neighbors, and coworkers notice a change in you as well. You no longer speak out against sin. Now you struggle to tell others about God's goodness to you and His love for them. Your heart is sad because you think you have hurt your Heavenly Father.

God knows you love Him, and He is not angry with you. Your heart's cry reaches God's ears and touches His heart. The fervent desire to please God and minister to others remains in you. Ask the Holy Spirit to rekindle the spark for God as never before. Your love for God and zeal to be His witness will burn brighter than ever!

TURN UP HIS VOICE IN YOUR HEART. ALLOW YOUR WITNESS TO SPEAK OF HIS GOODNESS IN YOUR LIFE.

JOY WILL COME

He renews our hopes and heals our bodies.

PSALM 147:3 CEV

How many times have you prayed with someone who has lost a loved one? You know the person is hurting, and you want to bring him or her some relief. What do you do? What do you say? Or perhaps you are the one experiencing such a loss.

There is no way to prepare for the pain of losing a loved one, but Your Heavenly Father can give you comfort. God knows the sadness death brings, and He is prepared to help you endure the hurt.

Talk to God about how you feel. Ask God to comfort you and help you comfort others.. Then think about the happy times spent with your loved one. That is what Jesus did when He knew that His friend Lazarus had died. Soon the feelings of sadness will be replaced joy. God will also give you the ability to support others as they grieve. You may be sad now, but Your Heavenly Father promises joy. Expect joy to return as you focus on God and His Word.

—∞∞—

WHILE ON THIS EARTH, JESUS WAS "A MAN OF SORROWS AND ACQUAINTED WITH GRIEF" (ISAIAH 53:3 NASB). HE KNOWS HOW TO COMFORT YOUR HEART IN EVERY SITUATION.

TIME OUT!

*In the morning, O LORD, you hear my voice; in the morning
I lay my requests before you and wait in expectation.*

PSALM 5:3 NIV

You wanted that executive-level job. You knew
you could handle the pressures that come with
being called "the boss." Sure, it would mean long
hours. Of course, there would be times of stress
and anxiety, but it comes with the territory.

Now, you realize the grass is not really as
green on the other side as you had imagined. The
hours ARE long. The meetings ARE endless. The
stress is REAL. You feel pulled in every direction,
and you are not handling it as well as you
expected.

There is one more meeting you should add to
your calendar—with your Heavenly Father. The
good thing is that you do not have to schedule an
appointment. God is always available—sitting in
the executive chair of His throne room waiting for
you. Go to God and ask Him to help you to get
your life in order. Tell God how much you need,
and want, His intervention. The Lord is ready and
willing to help you. The Lord is saying, "Give
your burdens to Me. I will bear them."

GOD NEVER LEAVES HIS CHILDREN IN NEED.
WHATEVER TASKS GOD PUTS BEFORE YOU, HE WILL
GIVE YOU THE STRENGTH TO HANDLE.

WHAT'S SO BAD ABOUT IT?

But each one is tempted when he is carried away and enticed by his own lust. Then when lust has conceived, it gives birth to sin; and when sin is accomplished, it brings forth death.

JAMES 1:14-15 NASB

It's just a movie, what can it hurt? I know the lyrics speak death and destruction, but I don't listen to the words anyway. I just like the music.

Excuses are the subtle tricks the devil uses to tempt you. But don't be fooled! It is the devil's job to make things look so attractive that you, as a Christian, would reason that nothing is wrong with them. But it is your responsibility to know the difference between right and wrong. It is also your duty to be watchful so that the enemy cannot trap you.

God said you are not ignorant when it comes to recognizing the evil plots of the devil—the traps that are designed to destroy you and your Christian testimony. How do you recognize evil? God's Word is the only measuring stick you need. If what you're looking at does not match up to what God's Word says, then stay away from it.

GOD'S WORD FIRMLY PLANTED IN YOUR HEART IS THE VERY WEAPON YOU NEED TO OVERCOME TEMPTATION, AND THE TEMPTER.

BETTER THAN YOU DESERVE

*Let us come before him with thanksgiving and
extol him with music and song.*

PSALM 95:2 NIV

*Nobody loves me. I never get anything I want.
Why do I always have it so hard?*

How often do you indulge in a pity party? Are you feeling alone, rejected, or left out? Or do you feel sorry for yourself because everyone around you seems to be doing so much better than you?

Stop it! Complaining never helps.

If you want something, then tell God about it. The Lord recognizes your voice, and He is ready to listen. God knows what is best for you. If your request benefits you, then God will see that you have it. Rest in the fact that God made you, and He knows what makes you happy. God knows what you need to fulfill His plan for your life.

For now, be thankful for what God has already done for you. Remind yourself of how many times God has proven himself by meeting your needs, answering your prayers, and giving you the secret desires of your heart. God knows what you need, and He knows what's best for you. God will see that you are cared for.

❧

COMPLAINING LEADS TO A DEAD END, BUT THANKFUL-
NESS BRINGS GOD'S GREATEST RESULTS.

INNER SANCTUM

*The fear of man brings a snare, but whoever leans on, trusts in,
and puts his confidence in the Lord is safe and set on high.*

PROVERBS 29:25 AMP

What are your first thoughts when you hear bad news? If you're like most people, then fear strikes. You worry that the same thing could happen to you or a loved one. That is not the response God expects from you. God expects you to remain calm and be at peace.

When you hear bad news, remind yourself that God is always there protecting you, your family, and your property. God promises to keep you in perfect peace; you never have to worry. Even when you face difficulty or danger, God promises to use the difficulties for good purposes.

The power that God provides for you is greater than any threat man can produce. When you begin to worry, draw from the power that is within you. In your heart, go to the secret place of safety that God provides and let Him fill you with peace. Trust God to keep His Word and keep you safe.

———

WHEN DANGER STRIKES, DO NOT PRESS THE PANIC
BUTTON. TALK TO GOD INSTEAD. LET THE LORD
USHER YOU INTO A PLACE OF PEACE WHERE WORRY
AND FEAR DO NOT RESIDE. TRUST GOD TO BE WITH
YOU AND TO PROTECT YOU.

SHOUT ABOUT IT!

*After they prayed, the place where they were meeting was
shaken. And they were all filled with the Holy Spirit and
spoke the word of God boldly.*

ACTS 4:31 NIV

If witnessing for Christ is hard for you, then ask
yourself why. Maybe you are afraid of rejection.
Possibly, you are a young Christian and do not feel
you are ready to talk intelligently about God with
others.

Your excuses might sound reasonable. However, the world must hear the Good News that
Jesus died for man's sin. The world must be told
that God stands ready to forgive sin and give new
life.

Whether you are a new believer or you have
been a Christian for some time, be confident that
God is with you at all times. God promises to
always be with us and never leave us alone. God's
Holy Spirit stands ready to be your mouthpiece;
you only need to trust the Lord.

GOD CALLS YOU TO BE A SPOKESPERSON FOR HIM.
GOD KNOWS WHAT TO SAY, EVEN WHEN YOU DO NOT.

THEY WON'T FORGET

Point your kids in the right direction—when they're old they won't be lost.

PROVERBS 22:6 MSG

Remember the joy you felt at the birth of your children? They depended on you for everything, and you were happy to oblige.

You still feel that way about your children, even though they are teenagers. But you also are living in fear—concerned that they will go down the wrong path and wind up in serious trouble.

Stop worrying about what might happen with your children, and start to consider all the good things that have already happened because of how you raised them. From their birth, you taught them about God's love as you protected and cared for them.

Today, as your children take the next step in the plan God has mapped out for them, continue to thank God for taking care of them. God knows all about the challenges they will face along the way, and He has promised to make sure they always have a way to escape. Do what you have always done—trust God.

WHEN YOUR CHILDREN ARE TEMPTED OR ARE
FACED WITH MAKING DIFFICULT DECISIONS THE LORD
WILL BE THERE TO HELP.

BE AT PEACE

*Try to live in peace with everyone, and seek to live a
clean and holy life.*

HEBREWS 12:14 NLT

It happened again. Someone said something to
hurt your feelings, and you didn't stand up for
yourself. Now that it is over, you wish you had
said something. At least you would have the satisfaction of knowing you made the other person
hurt, too.

However, as a Christian you know you can
never feel good about doing evil—no matter how
badly someone has hurt you.

If anyone ever had a reason to strike back, it
was Jesus. But rather than fight, His response to
cruelty was always love. Even as Jesus hung on the
Cross at Calvary, Jesus looked up to God and said,
"Father, forgive them." It takes strength and
courage to walk away from persecution, but you
can be like Jesus and choose to be a peacemaker.

You are a child of God and an heir with Jesus
Christ. That means you can respond just as Jesus
responds. Feeling hurt about something is just an
emotion, but that feeling doesn't stick around
forever. It is like a vapor that quickly disappears.

TRUST GOD TO AVENGE ANY WRONG DONE TO YOU.

AN HONEST DAY'S WORK

We worked hard day and night so that we would not be a burden to any of you.

2 THESSALONIANS 3:8 NLT

You considered all the options, and you still don't know which job would be right for you, or for your family. One job pays a lot more money than the other, but it means long hours away from your family. Your family could live comfortably with the salary from the other job, but what about vacations? Could you still afford to buy a new car and move into a better house?

First, make up your mind to obey God. Then, get rid of the stress and give the problem to the Lord. Do not allow money to make the decision for you, but place the responsibility for your decision where it rightfully belongs—in the hands of your Heavenly Father. God promises to bless the work of your hands and to see that you are successful. As your source, God always sees that your needs are met. The Lord provides for you by showing you how to use His wisdom in planning for the future.

———

GOD STANDS READY TO MAKE HIS WISDOM
AVAILABLE TO YOU.

NOT SEEING IS BELIEVING!

That is why we live by believing and not by seeing.

2 CORINTHIANS 5:7 NLT

*L*ord, *why was Abraham's faith so strong?* It is awesome that he trusted You to make Him a father when he was one hundred years old and when his wife, Sarah, was way past her childbearing years.

Abraham knew that it was impossible for him to impregnate his wife, Sarah. However, when God told Abraham that he and his wife would have a son, Abraham believed God. In other words, Abraham took God at His word.

Abraham put aside his natural understanding and trusted God's spoken promise. Abraham's faith honored God, and God blessed Abraham in return. As a result, Sarah gave birth to Isaac according to God's promise (Genesis 21:1-2).

Likewise, God sent Gabriel to tell Mary that she would bear God's Son by the Holy Spirit. Mary was to name the child Jesus. Mary simply believed God's promise, and our Savior was born (Luke 1:26-38).

AS YOU READ GOD'S WORD, BELIEVE THAT GOD IS TALKING TO YOU PERSONALLY. REJOICE AS YOUR FAITH INCREASES.

TOO HEAVY TO CARRY

"I won't lay anything heavy or ill-fitting on you. Keep company
with me and you'll learn to live freely and lightly."

MATTHEW 11:29-30 MSG

You always feel confident in your abilities. Usually, you are the first to volunteer on a new project. When others give up, you persevere. Now, however, your boss gives you a major assignment, and you are overwhelmed.

Why me, Lord? Why me?

Stop for a minute. Remember that you are a child of a loving God who always takes care of His children, and you are not alone in this situation.

Most likely, your doubt results from a fear that you might fail. Confess your fear of failure. Tell the Lord you want to do a good job, but you need His help.

Not only does God care about you, but He also cares about everything that affects you. If God trusts you enough to give you this assignment, then He will be there to help you carry it out. No weight is too heavy for the Lord.

WHENEVER SOMETHING IS TOO HEAVY FOR
YOU TO BEAR, TAKE COMFORT IN KNOWING THAT
GOD WILL CARRY IT FOR YOU.

YOUR NEXT MOVE

*My dear friends, you should be quick to listen and
slow to speak.*

JAMES 1:19 CEV

Have you ever made a quick decision because
you had a "gut" feeling and discovered later
that you did not have all the facts? It is not a very
comfortable place to be, especially if you learn
your decision was a wrong one.

You can be sure your decisions are right if you
pray and ask God for direction. Basing decisions
on what you feel or think leaves too much room
for error. But you will not go wrong if you trust
God for direction.

Not only does He know all things and see
much further than you, God doesn't make
mistakes. God does not have "gut" reactions.

Next time, take an extra moment before
making a decision and pray. Expect to hear from
your heavenly Father who promises to light your
path.

———

WHEN YOUR UNDERSTANDING IS LIMITED, DON'T BE
QUICK TO MAKE A DECISION. LISTEN CAREFULLY AND
LET GOD SHOW YOU WHAT TO SAY OR DO.

JUST WHAT THE DOCTOR ORDERED

Jesus traveled through all the cities and villages of that area, teaching in the synagogues and announcing the Good News about the Kingdom. And wherever he went, he healed people of every sort of disease and illness.

MATTHEW 9:35 NLTT

You're sick. At first, you wonder what the source of your illness is. But then you reflect on your lifestyle over the last several years and conclude you have not given your body the proper care and nourishment it needed.

The devil uses "sneak attacks" like sickness to knock you off track and to keep you from doing the work God has assigned to you. But God provides an instant cure through the healing power of His Word (Proverbs 4:22 AMP). His Word is an antidote to disease. When administered properly—studied and applied in your life—the Word works to keep your body healthy. So use the Word of God.

IF YOU ARE FACED WITH SICKNESS BECAUSE YOU HAVE NEGLECTED TAKING CARE OF YOUR BODY, THEN BE HONEST WITH GOD AND CONFESS.

GOD KNOWS BEST

I am the LORD your God, who teaches you what is best for you, who directs you in the way you should go.

ISAIAH 48:17 NIV

It is wise to prepare for the future. But prepare knowing that you can also rely on God's blessings if you are following His plan.

How many times have you looked expectantly for something to happen, only to be disappointed when it never materialized? Just because something looks good, sounds good, or feels good does not mean it is good for you. There is nothing wrong with planning for the future. The Bible tells us that the ant carefully prepares for the future by storing food (Proverbs 6:6). It is only when you do not include God that your plans are wrong.

When you ask Him, God will special attention to your needs. As you pray, God directs your steps so that you don't get lost or confused. God sees that you are never disappointed.

———

WHEN THINGS DO NOT GO THE
WAY YOU EXPECT, RECOGNIZE THAT GOD'S HAND
IS GUIDING YOUR FUTURE.

HELLO, NEIGHBOR!

Who may worship in your sanctuary, LORD? Who may enter
your presence on your holy hill? Those who lead blameless lives
and do what is right, speaking the truth from sincere hearts.
Those who refuse to slander others or harm their neighbors
or speak evil of their friends.

PSALM 15:1-3 NLT

Do you have neighbors who make you feel slightly uncomfortable? Maybe you do not understand or agree with their lifestyle. Before unkind thoughts grab hold of your mind, pray and allow the Holy Spirit to lead you into God's presence.

Let God's peace settle your mind. The Lord hears your prayers, and He knows your concerns.

Rely on God's love to help you control negative thoughts and behave kindly. God's compassion helps you see past faults so that you can pray about your neighbors' needs. Ask for wisdom and trust God to help you understand other people. Only then will you be free to love your neighbor as well as witness for Jesus Christ.

IF YOU HAVE A NEIGHBOR THAT YOU ARE
UNCOMFORTABLE WITH, THEN TRUST GOD AND PRAY
FOR OPPORTUNITIES TO WITNESS FOR HIM.

WHERE ARE YOU, LORD?

Do not banish me from your presence,
and don't take your Holy Spirit from me.

PSALM 51:11 NLT

Something does not feel right. You have been praying, reading God's Word, and praising God, but you do not sense His presence.

You love the Lord with all your heart. He is your life—your everything. The feeling of being separated from Him is more than you can bear. You begin to understand how the separation from God that Jesus experienced on the cross might have been more agonizing than the actual crucifixion.

The quiet moments when you feel far from God are wonderful opportunities to remember His love and loyal devotion to you. Because of your love for God, it is easy to remember His provision, protection, and comfort for you. Soon, you will lose track of time thinking about God's goodness to you.

———

GOD IS GREATER THAN THE WORLD AGAINST YOU,
AND HE IS ON YOUR SIDE. YOU CAN TRUST GOD TO
NEVER LEAVE YOU ALONE.

TURN IT AROUND!

*And we know that God causes everything to work together
for the good of those who love God and are called according to
his purpose for them.*

ROMANS 8:28 NLT

Do you feel that you have made so many
mistakes that there is no need to expect
anything good from you? Perhaps it seems that no
matter how hard you try to please God and help
others something goes wrong.

The Bible contains many examples of how
God transforms weakness to strength and
foolishness to wisdom. Abraham, Moses, David,
Samson, and Paul are among them. God's Word
reveals that even when they disobeyed God, He
forgave them and graciously turned some of their
mistakes into great victories.

Your sincere and humble heart desires to
please God and bless others. No matter what kind
of mistakes you make, God forgives you and turns
things around for your good. You are on your way
to a successful and rewarding life of doing
wonderful things for God.

EVERYTHING GOD CREATES IS GOOD—
INCLUDING YOU.

JUST LIKE HIM

*And as the Spirit of the Lord works within us, we become more
and more like him and reflect his glory even more.*

2 CORINTHIANS 3:18 NLT

Not all Christians act like Christ Jesus did when He walked the earth. Every Christian is a work in progress. We are shaped and molded daily by God's hand.

Be encouraged because God created you to be like Him. You are His child, vitally connected to Him, and living in Him. His Word describes you as a fruitful branch (John 15:4 AMP) and a flourishing tree of righteousness (Isaiah 61:3 KJV). Your fruit reveals your spiritual growth and maturity. As God's child, you continue to mature in your Christian walk regardless of your age or the number of years you have been a Christian. So do not try to grow up fast or compare yourself with other Christians. Your Heavenly Father loves you and is pleased with who you are.

BECOMING CHRIST-LIKE IS INEVITABLE WHEN
YOU SPEND TIME WORSHIPING, STUDYING
GOD'S WORD, AND PRAYING.

OVER THE LIMIT

*So then, whether you eat or drink, or whatever you may do, do
all for the honor and glory of God.*

1 CORINTHIANS 10:31 AMP

*W*here did those bulges come from? You stare
at your reflection in the bathroom mirror.
Timidly, you step on the bathroom scale, and it
verifies what you saw in the mirror. This will never
do because you are planning to attend the staff
Christmas and New Year's Eve parties.

*Dear Lord, please help me. Forgive me for
being proud and selfish and forgetting that my
body is Your temple. I want to be healthy, feel
good, and look good for Your glory.*

Your Heavenly Father hears you. God is there
to comfort you. The Lord's wisdom will reveal to
you and your doctor the perfect method for
achieving a healthy weight. God will give you the
patience to persevere. And the Holy Spirit will help
you restore godly discipline and balance to every
area of your life.

GOD'S WISDOM AND HIS HOLY SPIRIT WILL EMPOWER
YOU TO ESTABLISH AND MAINTAIN GODLY HABITS.
DISCIPLINE AND SELF-CONTROL ARE NECESSARY FOR A
HEALTHY LIFESTYLE THAT GLORIFIES GOD.

ALONE BUT NOT ABANDONED

The Lord will not abandon his chosen people, for that would dishonor his great name. He made you a special nation for himself—just because he wanted to!

1 SAMUEL 12:22 TLB

For years, you enjoyed the pleasures that came with marriage. In good times, there was always a companion to share in your joy. In difficult times, you comforted one another with words of encouragement. When you needed a friend, your spouse was always there.

Suddenly, you are divorced and alone. Abandoned! What do you do?

Tell God how you feel. His Son experienced feelings of loneliness and abandonment as He hung on the cross. For awhile, Jesus felt abandoned and cried out to God: "Why have you forsaken me?" God had not left Jesus alone. And neither are you alone. When everybody else walks away and leaves you standing alone, God will never leave your side. As your Heavenly Father, He will fill the emptiness in your life instantly.

SHAKE OFF THOSE FEELINGS OF ABANDONMENT
AND TALK WITH THE ONE WHO TRULY LOVES YOU.

DON'T GIVE IN!

*So be subject to God. Resist the devil [stand firm against him],
and he will flee from you.*

JAMES 4:7 AMP

In the years since you became a Christian, you have found it easy to say "no" to the things that you know are wrong. But for some strange reason, this "great opportunity" seems too good to pass up. The voice inside you keeps saying, "No, don't do it!" Yet you are so drawn. Why?

Thank God for His Holy Spirit. The Holy Spirit keeps you from yielding to temptation. Thankfully, the Spirit of God and His Word are at work in you to keep you from falling into the devil's trap.

When you pray, the Holy Spirit inside of you directs your mind and your heart. The Spirit gives you the strength to resist the devil's temptations. God's Word is hidden in your heart where the enemy cannot steal it. Use God's Word as a shield to ward off those fiery darts of temptation when they come. The Word will extinguish the temptations so that they don't become a "consuming fire."

IT IS GOOD TO KNOW THAT YOUR HEAVENLY FATHER
WATCHES OVER YOU. THANK GOD FOR BEING YOUR
HELP IN TIMES OF TROUBLE.

STANDING IN THE GAP

Confess to one another therefore your faults [your slips, your false steps, your offenses, your sins] and pray [also] for one another, that you may be healed and restored [to a spiritual tone of mind and heart]. The earnest (heartfelt, continued) prayer of a righteous man makes tremendous power available [dynamic in its working].

JAMES 5:16 AMP

You are really concerned about your friend and try so hard to help, but nothing seems to help. Your friend's addiction is such a stronghold, and there seems to be no solution.

Thank God that His Word promises to rescue us from the kingdom of darkness and bring us into the light. In other words, God's Word provides a way of escape for your friend. The Bible enables us to withstand all attacks—sickness, disease, poverty, or addiction.

God says our weapons are not things we can see, touch, or feel—they are spiritual weapons. The opposition cannot win against the weapons God gives us. Prayer is one of God's weapons, and He has given you prayer to use whenever attacks come. Use prayer to fight for your friend, and thank God that your friend can have the victory.

WHEN TROUBLE COMES AGAINST A FRIEND, OR
ANYONE YOU CARE ABOUT, REMEMBER THAT GOD
HAS ARMED YOU WITH POWERFUL WEAPONS.

GIVE OR TAKE

For we all often stumble and fall and offend in many things.
And if anyone does not offend in speech [never says the wrong
things], he is a fully developed character and a perfect man,
able to control his whole body and to curb his entire nature.

JAMES 3:2 AMP

Someone offended you—did something that hurt your feelings and made you angry. And now your response has offended them. But neither giving offense nor taking offense shows God's love. God wants you to control your feelings so that they do not cause you to sin (Hebrews 5:14 AMP).

Ask God to help you fix the problems caused by yielding to the offense. God wants you to share His love with those who mistreat you. Ask God to help you resist giving or taking offense. Then God's love will shine through you. If there are certain "buttons" in your life that spark anger when pushed, then ask God to help you get rid of those buttons. Be thankful that He loves you in spite of your shortcomings, and He will help you forgive the shortcomings of others.

GIVING AND RECEIVING OFFENSE KEEPS YOU IN
BONDAGE. GOD GIVES YOU THE KEY AND WAITS FOR
YOU TO UNLOCK THE DOOR.

DON'T SWEAT IT!

Give your entire attention to what God is doing right now, and don't get worked up about what may or may not happen tomorrow. God will help you deal with whatever hard things come up when the time comes.

MATTHEW 6:34 MSG

Stop the world, I want to get off!
It is easy to feel overwhelmed. One more thing and you think you will explode. Your frustration is a clear sign of anxiety, pressure, and stress creeping into your life. Stop and rest. That is what Jesus did when He grew tired (Mark 4:39). Jesus gave the same advice to His disciples when they were tired from ministering to the crowds of people (Mark 6:31).

Do not let the cares of tomorrow stress you out today. God knows how busy you are, and He promises to help you. Follow Jesus' example and give your body the rest it needs. Your Heavenly Father wants what is best for you. God helps you work and rest so that you are healthy, strong, and able to enjoy life.

———

DECIDE TO TAKE TIME TO REST AND
MEDITATE ON GOD'S PROMISES.

A LIGHT BURDEN

*I took the world off your shoulders, freed you from
a life of hard labor.*

PSALM 81:6 MSG

You have faced difficulty before, and each time
your faith in God delivers you from harm.
This time it's different. The burden of praying for
someone else is such a weight that now you feel as
oppressed as the person you are praying for.

Bearing one another's burdens is an act of
obedience to God and His Word (Galatians 6), but
it can result in you feeling the weight of that
person's problems. Jesus says His yoke is easy and
His burden is light. When you place the person
you are praying for in His hands, God becomes
responsible for the burden. And for God, the
burden is light and easy to manage.

So go ahead, pray for your friend's problem.
Give it to God so that your hands can be lifted in
praise to Him. Also, your hands are then free to
do everything else that God gives you.

TAKE THE WORLD OFF YOUR SHOULDERS AND PLACE
IT WHERE IT BELONGS—WITH THE ONE WHO KNOWS
JUST HOW TO CARRY SUCH A LOAD.

EQUIPPED FOR BATTLE

Put on the full armor of God.

EPHESIANS 6:13 NIV

When you asked Christ Jesus to be your Lord, God clothed you with garments of salvation and the robe of righteousness (Isaiah 61:10). But God knew that you would encounter opposition so He equipped you with supernatural armor to fight the good fight of faith and protect you from the enemy. Furthermore, God instructed you on your armor's purpose and how to use it.

As you trust God and stand firm, He will bring you through every difficulty. God provides everything you need to prepare for life's challenges. You can confidently and boldly face trouble and opposition knowing that the Lord, who is strong and mighty in battle, has prepared you for victory.

God is on your side, and He has overcome the world (John 16:33).

YOU ARE MORE THAN A CONQUEROR THROUGH JESUS CHRIST—NOTHING CAN DEFEAT YOU. YOU ARE READY FOR BATTLE!

QUALITY TIME

*Listen to my voice in the morning, LORD. Each morning
I bring my requests to you and wait expectantly.*

PSALM 5:3 NLT

You want to spend more time with God. But with the many demands that are placed on you every day—your family, your job, and even church duties—there is just never enough time for true worship or fellowship.

The Bible says the spirit is willing, but the flesh is weak. Weakness can lead to failure. Tell God how you struggle and fail when it comes to spending time with Him. Let God know how much you love Him and want that time of fellowship. If you need strength, God promises to be your strength when you are weak. In fact, God said His strength becomes perfect in weakness.

God will point out the things that are keeping you from spending time with Him. The Lord will also help you plan your day so that you never miss time with Him.

———

SPENDING QUALITY TIME WITH GOD EVERY DAY
STRENGTHENS YOUR FAITH IN HIM.

THE COURAGE TO SPEAK UP

You must go wherever I send you and say whatever I tell you.
And don't be afraid of the people, for I will be with you and
take care of you. I, the LORD, have spoken!

JEREMIAH 1:7-8 NLT

You wanted to say something, but you remained silent. You wonder if those around you, those who looked up to you for support, have lost confidence in you. You are embarrassed to admit you felt so intimidated that you could not look your supervisors in the eye.

Going up against management can be scary. The fear of reprimand or getting fired is frightening. But the Lord, who is always with you, will tell you what to say. God offers the same encouragement to you as He did to Joshua: "Be strong and of good courage, do not fear nor be afraid of them; for the LORD your God, He is the One who goes with you. He will not leave you nor forsake you" (Deuteronomy 31:6 NKJV).

GOD WILL GIVE YOU THE COURAGE TO FACE
OBSTACLES AND OVERCOME THEM.

I Can Hardly Wait!

No eye has seen, no ear has heard, and no mind has imagined what God has prepared for those who love him.

1 Corinthians 2:9 NLT

Where will I be, and what will I be doing ten years from now?

How will I spend the rest of my life?

Each of us asks these questions at one time or another, but seldom do we have all the answers. Chances are we have already mapped out some kind or plan for our lives, but do our plans line up with what God has planned for us?

Because you were created by God, only He knows your destiny. God planned your future before you were ever born, but what a joy to know that God's plan includes a successful future (Jeremiah 29:11). Look back over the path that you have walked and see that God has led you every step of the way. And He's still guiding you today.

Don't spend your days concerned about tomorrow. Enjoy the element of surprise when you see what God does in your life.

EVER FAITHFUL

Yet I still dare to hope when I remember this: The unfailing love of the LORD never ends! By his mercies we have been kept from complete destruction. Great is his faithfulness; his mercies begin afresh each day.

LAMENTATIONS 3:21-23 NLT

Not another one! Your latest book proposal is rejected for the third time. There's plenty of room here for self-pity, you think. Instead you reach for your Bible, seeking encouragement and an assurance that you are not alone. And you're not!

In the Old Testament, King David encouraged himself by meditating on God's promises instead of indulging in self-pity. David remembered that God never forsook His children. David realized that God's people never lacked any good thing when they obeyed Him.

Just as God was there for David, He is here for you. Hold on to your dreams. God is your source, and He can take care of you in every situation. Praise Him for what He has already done for you and thank Him for meeting every need that arises.

WHEN YOU TRUST IN GOD, YOU CAN BE STRONG
IN TIMES OF REJECTION AND DISAPPOINTMENT.

A LIVING LETTER

Clearly, you are a letter from Christ prepared by us. It is written not with pen and ink, but with the Spirit of the living God. It is carved not on stone, but on human hearts.

2 CORINTHIANS 3:3 NLT

You are the only Jesus some people will ever see.

You realize the importance of this statement when you see the negative influences in the world—like drugs, alcohol, violence, and illicit sex. You are thankful for God's salvation, and you know that He keeps you from temptation. More than ever, you want others to know about the saving love of Jesus. Every day you ask the Lord to help you show them His love in some way. You realize that it is your responsibility to share the Good News in your words and actions.

You know God's desire to see people saved, and He will show you how to be His witness. God can use you as a living Bible for people to "read" and come to Him.

THE BIBLE IS GOD'S WORD, WRITTEN IN BLACK AND WHITE. YOU ARE HIS LIVING WITNESS WHOSE LIFE OTHERS CAN SEE AND COME TO GOD.

BE THANKFUL FOR THAT?

Thank [God] in everything [no matter what the circumstances may be, be thankful and give thanks], for this is the will of God for you [who are] in Christ Jesus [the Revealer and Mediator of that will].

1 THESSALONIANS 5:18 AMP

Your day begins with a sweet time of fellowship with God in worship and prayer. But then everything falls apart. You burn breakfast, lose the car keys, and get a flat tire. Perhaps you need to pray some more.

You face challenges every day, and they can make you angry, frustrated, discouraged, or embarrassed. So, how do you handle it? Your time talking to your heavenly Father prepares you for your day—no matter what you face. Your Heavenly Father walks with you through the challenges of the day so that you keep your peace, joy, composure, and sanity. God empowers you with the strength to refuse to give up. Knowing that God loves you and takes care of you brings songs of thanksgiving to your lips. Your God is bigger than life!

YOUR GRATITUDE GLORIFIES AND PLEASES GOD.
THANKFULNESS MINIMIZES THE STRESS AND
MAXIMIZES YOUR JOY.

THE RIGHT ONE

*Can two people walk together without agreeing
on the direction?*

AMOS 3:3 NLT

Life's opportunities require you to make choices
every day. Good or bad, right or wrong, in or
out, up or down, front or back, top or bottom,
black or white—the choices are endless. Some
people think they can compromise, but that gets
them nowhere.

If you are confused or hesitant about making a
decision, then get quiet before God. No matter
how good an idea seems, step into God's presence
before making a decision. Confusion will hinder
you from hearing and obeying God. And the Lord
said being double-minded will keep your prayers
from being answered.

Listen to God. Allow Him to quiet your mind
so that you can hear His voice. Then you will
choose what is right, and God will guarantee your
success.

SOMETIMES KNOWING GOOD FROM BAD SEEMS EASY,
BUT GOD WANTS THE BEST FOR YOU. THAT IS WHY
GOD DIRECTS YOU ALONG THE RIGHT PATH RATHER
THAN THAT WHICH IS ONLY GOOD.

LIFTED UP

But You, O LORD, are a shield around me, my glory, and the one who lifts my head high.

PSALM 3:3 NLT

For the hundredth time you encourage yourself saying, "What's done is done. I admit I was wrong. I wish that I could go back and undo it, but I can't. God has forgiven me, and as far as I am concerned life goes on, and by His grace so do I."

Enough time has passed that you feel brave enough to leave the comfort of your home and resume your life. The vivid picture of the shock on people's faces replays across your mind. You still hear the disgust and contempt in their voices, even from family members. Guilt almost chokes you as you drop your head in shame like a child being scolded by his parents.

Christ Jesus suffered pain and shame when He was crucified for you. Almighty God has forgiven you and restored you to a place of fellowship with himself through Jesus' sacrifice. He lifts you up and crowns you with glory and honor (Psalm 8:5). God is not ashamed of you (Hebrews 2:11). Now lift your head and your heart with praise to the One who loves you with an everlasting love.

WHEN YOU DO WRONG, RUN TO GOD—NOT AWAY FROM HIM. THE LORD WILL FORGIVE YOU AND LIFT YOUR BURDEN OF GUILT.

HOME, SWEET HOME

Through skillful and godly Wisdom is a house (a life, a home, a family) built, and by understanding it is established [on a sound and good foundation].

PROVERBS 24:3 AMP

Your heart is troubled because your family is not getting along with each other. You and your spouse are either touchy or distant, and your children are moody and complain about little things. Busy schedules prevent conversation, and you cannot remember the last time you sat down to a family dinner. If you are unhappy about it, then God is too.

And the Lord desires that you and your family grow closer to each other and to Him. When you put your family in His hands, God will point out the areas you need to work on. God's wisdom will guide you, and the Holy Spirit will empower you. As you allow God to help you rebuild with His love, your home will be a haven of joy, peace, laughter, companionship, and togetherness. You will enjoy each other as God walks and talks with you.

ONLY GOD CAN MAKE PEOPLE INTO A FAMILY AND A HOUSE INTO A HOME. GOD'S PRESENCE AND LOVE MAKE THE DIFFERENCE.

A FLICKER OF LIGHT

He has rescued us from the dominion of darkness and brought us into the kingdom of the Son.

COLOSSIANS 1:13 NIV

Does darkness seem to hover over your life? Perhaps fear, oppression, or ominous thoughts cloud your mind. In a dark room you turn on a light, click on a flashlight, or light a candle. When emotional or spiritual darkness feels overwhelming, remember that one flicker of God's light dispels the darkness.

Just as you reach for a light switch in the darkness, you can reach for God's light—His presence, power, and strength. When He dwells within you, darkness can not stay. Remind yourself, *I don't have to give into the darkness because God is with me.*

Ephesians 5:8 NASB says we "were formerly darkness, but now [we] are Light in the Lord; walk as children of Light." Never forget that God has rescued you from darkness! The light of God's love shines out from His children. Although God may reveal His goodness through caring people, the light of His presence is the best gift of all.

WHEN WORRY AND DESPAIR CLOUD YOUR MIND, YOU CAN SAY WITH THE PSALMIST, "THE LORD IS MY LIGHT AND MY SALVATION; WHOM SHALL I FEAR? THE LORD IS THE STRENGTH OF MY LIFE; OF WHOM SHALL I BE AFRAID?" (PSALM 27:1 NKJV).

MORE THAN BEFORE

*Instead of shame and dishonor, you will inherit a double
portion of prosperity and everlasting joy.*

ISAIAH 61:7 NLT

L oss can cause hurt and pain. In addition, loss
creates feelings of vulnerability, hopelessness,
and helplessness. Whether you feel threatened with
the possibility of loss or have already experienced
loss, the despair seems hard to overcome. Perhaps
you feel like you are on an emotional rollercoaster
as you try to make sense of what happened. Hurt
and anger prompt questions like, "Lord, why did
You let this happen to me?" Regardless of the circumstances, your Heavenly Father's grace is
available to strengthen you and bring restoration.

For example, in the Old Testament, Job was a
man of integrity who loved God and hated evil.
But Job lost his health, children, and property.
Later, God gave Job more blessings than he had
before his tragic loss (Job 42:12-16).

The Lord can do the same for you. God is no
respecter of persons, and He does not change.
Many wonderful blessings are yet to come.

TODAY'S SUFFERING CANNOT COMPARE TO
TOMORROW'S VICTORY IN GOD. GOD ADDS AND
MULTIPLIES BLESSINGS FOR YOU THAT FAR OUTWEIGH
YOUR LOSS.

STOP THE ABUSE!

*He delivered me from my powerful enemies, from those
who hated me and were too strong for me. They attacked me
at a moment when I was weakest, but the LORD upheld me.
He led me to a place of safety; he rescued me because
he delights in me.*

PSALM 18:17-19 NLT

You trust these people, and you cannot believe
they could hurt and humiliate you like this!
They apologize, and you forgive them. After all,
people make mistakes, and they promise not to do
it again—but they have, in fact, several times. You
wonder if unconsciously you have done something
to deserve this treatment.

Your Heavenly Father loves you so much that
He allowed His Son, Jesus, to die for you. God's
sweet and tender compassion would never cause
Him to mistreat you in any way. You are precious
to God's heart, and your welfare concerns Him.
The Lord leads and protects you. The healing balm
of God's presence will soothe your wounds. The
Lord will restore your peace and dignity.

GOD'S LOVE BUILDS YOU UP. THE LORD CROWNS
YOU WITH HONOR AND GLORY SO THAT YOU CAN
ENJOY ABUNDANT LIFE.

FREE AT LAST!

In [this] freedom Christ has made us free [and completely liberated us]; stand fast then, and do not be hampered and held ensnared and submit again to a yoke of slavery [which you have once put off].

GALATIANS 5:1 AMP

It started with just a little here and there. But soon it began to snowball, and you found yourself out of control. What you considered simple and innocent grew into a powerful force. Willpower is no longer enough, and you have become a slave to addiction. You cry to be set free.

God hears your cry, and His compassion will not fail you. Your deliverance begins when you confess that your life is no longer your own. Indeed, your life is not your own because you live in God. When you became a Christian, the Lord freed you from the bondage of sin and gave you power.

God's love for you is still the same, and so is His desire for you to be free. As you reach up to God, He will pull you out of the mire and set your feet on the solid rock of Jesus Christ. With God's help you can stand free.

ADDICTIONS KEEP YOU IN BONDAGE. YOUR HEAVENLY FATHER LONGS TO BREAK THE CHAINS OF ADDICTION SO THAT YOU CAN WORSHIP HIM IN FREEDOM.

THE PAST IS PAST

*He lifted me out of the pit of despair, out of the mud
and the mire. He set my feet on solid ground and steadied me
as I walked along.*

PSALM 40:2 NLT

You've tried to succeed in life. But it seems that around every corner there is some reminder of your past: a high-school dropout, a failed marriage, a former prison inmate begging on a street corner. It is all too much of a reminder that your life spells F-A-I-L-U-R-E.

You need to change your address and move into the present. Guilt and shame remind you of your past, but God focuses on your future. Look where you're headed. God has a plan filled with hope.

Start thanking God that He has redeemed you from a terrible life of sin and failure. Now along with the Apostle Paul you can say, "but one thing I do: forgetting what lies behind and reaching forward to what lies ahead, I press on toward the goal for the prize of the upward call of God in Christ Jesus (Philippians 3:13-14 NASB)."

See your life as Paul saw his—a past that was dead and a future filled with life and promise.

YOUR PAST IS BEHIND YOU. GOD DOES NOT LIVE
THERE AND NEITHER SHOULD YOU.

THE ANSWER IS ON THE WAY

I say to you: Ask and it will be given to you; seek and you will find; knock and the door will be opened to you. For everyone who asks receives; he who seeks finds; and to him who knocks, the door will be opened.

LUKE 11:9-10 NIV

As a child, you were not afraid to ask your parents for something. You were confident that they would provide for your needs because of their love for you.

Now, you fear that it is different to ask God for something. But is it?

The Bible says that your Heavenly Father expects you to come to Him with the confidence that whatever you ask according to His will, He will do. That means you don't have to be afraid. You don't have to beg, and you don't have to grovel.

God is a loving Father who hears and answers His children's cry. God says, "I will answer; and while they are still speaking, I will hear" (Isaiah 65:24 NKJV). The Lord invites you to "fearlessly and confidently and boldly draw near to the throne of grace" (Hebrews 4:16 AMP).

———

WHATEVER YOUR NEED IS TODAY, GO TO GOD JUST AS YOU WOULD GO TO A LOVING PARENT. TALK TO GOD AND YOUR PRAYERS WILL RECEIVE HIS UNDIVIDED ATTENTION.

THE RIGHT WAY TO GIVE

*Every man shall give as he is able, according to the blessing of
the LORD your God which He has given you.*

DEUTERONOMY 16:17 NKJV

What motivates you to give? The desire to get
something in return motivates some people
to give. But God said in His Word that it is better
to give than to receive.

Others give because they feel pressured or
believe that giving is "the right thing to do." The
Bible says you should never give reluctantly or
because of pressure. Instead, you must make up
your own mind as to how much you should give
and do it cheerfully.

Love is the proper motivation for giving. God
demonstrates the proper motivation for giving
with the gift of His Son as a ransom for mankind.

When you give out of love, you are imitating
Your Heavenly Father. God promises that your gift
will be returned to you in a greater measure than
what you gave. God promises to supply all your
needs. That's your reward for giving out of a heart
of love.

THINK OF GIVING AS A GIFT YOU GIVE TO GOD.

LET IT GO!

I am overcome with joy because of your unfailing love,
for you have seen my troubles, and you care about the anguish
of my soul.

PSALM 31:7 NLT

Ever notice that when it comes to forgiveness you are harder on yourself than on others? You keep beating yourself down about your past mistakes.

You are a new person when you become a born-again Christian. Your mind is renewed, and your life is transformed. Now that you are a member of God's family, your past is blotted out. In fact, God said that He takes all your confessed sins and casts them as far away as the east is from the west. He does not remember them, and neither should you.

Perhaps you have trouble forgiving yourself because you don't trust yourself. You may think, "I'll just do it again and again." Don't think like that. Instead, thank God for wiping your slate clean. His Holy Spirit helps you resist sin. But, His wonderful grace and mercy forgive you when you do sin.

EVERYBODY DESERVES A SECOND CHANCE.
DO NOT WASTE TIME WORRYING ABOUT A PAST THAT
NO LONGER EXISTS.

THE TESTIMONY OF MARRIAGE

Give honor to marriage, and remain faithful to one another in marriage. God will surely judge people who are immoral and those who commit adultery.

HEBREWS 13:4 NLT

You thank God for your mate and your marriage. Your fervent prayer is that it will be an example for your children of the loving relationship between Jesus Christ and the Church. You pray that your children watch how you love God and one another. You hope that they allow your marriage to be a pattern for theirs. And particularly, you want them to remember how you prayed and held onto God and each other during hardship.

As you teach your children the importance of abstaining from sexual involvement before marriage, thank God that they will resist temptation. Trust God's grace and mercy to keep your children and their future mates away from temptation. Then your children will experience the joy and peace of a godly marriage.

GOD DESIRES THAT YOUR MARRIAGE, AS WELL AS YOUR CHILDREN'S MARRIAGES, BE TESTIMONIES OF HIS LOVE.

ALL BRAND NEW

Put on the new man which was created according to God,
in true righteousness and holiness.

EPHESIANS 4:24 NKJV

Everything that God created was good. But sin entered the earth and perverted man's mind. Now, the devil uses evil to tempt man and lure man from God.

Thank God that He cleaned you by the blood of Christ Jesus. You are born again—His new creation. The Holy Spirit leads you to think, see, talk, and walk like God. God loves you, and you love Him. The Holy Spirit's presence inside you gives you the strength to boldly say no to temptation.

As you pray and stay in His presence, your mind is renewed. You enjoy godly living. You no longer want to conform to the world's way of doing things, but you want to live for God. You delight that those who remember the old you do not recognize the new you. And now, your heart's desire is to show others how they can be given a new life—a blessed and holy life for all eternity.

———

THANK GOD FOR BEING THERE TO GUIDE YOU
AS YOU STRIVE TO BE MORE LIKE HIM.

I MISS YOU!

*Precious in the sight of the LORD is the death of
His godly ones.*

PSALM 116:15 NASB

It seems that time stood still when the doctor said
you lost your baby. You have cried so much that
it seems that your well of tears is running dry. The
visitors and callers have almost stopped coming to
visit, and now you are faced with emptiness and
despair.

You have a loving Heavenly Father who is
gracious and full of compassion. God understands
your pain and emptiness. Your little one belongs to
the Lord, too. In the midst of the grief, God offers
you comfort and hope. There is comfort in
knowing that your precious one is perfectly happy
and healthy with Him. Though your arms ache to
hold your baby, feel God's presence as He wraps
His arms around the both of you. You are His
child so let the Lord sing you a sweet lullaby as
you lay your head to rest on Him.

Just take all the time that you need to heal.
Daily, let God's presence bring peace to your
wounded heart.

LIKE YOU, GOD LOST HIS CHILD FOR A TIME WHEN
JESUS DIED ON THE CROSS FOR THE SINS OF THE
WORLD. BUT NOW, GOD AND HIS SON ARE TOGETHER
FOREVER ENJOYING EACH OTHER IN HEAVEN.

GUARANTEED VICTORY

The Lord will fight for you, and you shall hold your peace and remain at rest.

EXODUS 14:14 AMP

It just does not seem fair that when people treat you badly, you still have to love them. Sometimes you would rather give them a piece of your mind and be done with it.

That is the way the world thinks. But you are not of the world, and God does not want you thinking like the world. Since you made Jesus the Lord of your life, the Bible says you have the mind of Christ. Now you want to act like Jesus acts, think like Jesus thinks, and talk like Jesus talks.

What did Jesus say when the Roman soldiers nailed Him to the cross? Jesus asked God to forgive them because the soldiers did not know what they were doing. Those who are oppressing you do not understand what they are doing either. You are God's child, and they are mistreating you. Without realizing it, they are also mistreating your Heavenly Father. And like any loving father, God will come to the rescue of His child.

NOT EVERY OFFENSE IS WORTH A FIGHT—ESPECIALLY
WHEN YOU HAVE A FATHER WHO IS READY TO TAKE
ON YOUR ENEMIES. LOVE AND FORGIVE YOUR ENEMY.

ALWAYS TOGETHER

No, I will not abandon you as orphans—I will come to you.

JOHN 14:18 NLT

You know what it feels like to be lonely. But never before have you felt the emptiness you are feeling right now. Everyone you call is either not at home, or they're too busy to talk. Even the dog seems like he's not interested in you.

In today's fast-paced world it is not surprising that people do not have time for each other. Thankfully, God is not that way. His schedule may be full, but God always has time to fit in one more person, listen to one more problem, and calm one more fear. That is because God's love for you is the same now as it was when He allowed Jesus to die for you. God still wants a father-to-child relationship with you.

God's Spirit is inside of you. When you acknowledge the Lord's presence, He responds by giving you His peace. Suddenly, your emptiness is replaced with deep satisfaction. The realization of His love is alive inside you, and you begin to sense His presence. God provides you with peace of mind as He has promised (John 14:27).

LONELINESS IS EASILY OVERCOME WHEN
YOU MEDITATE ON GOD'S LOVE AND
FAITHFULNESS TO YOU.

No Looking Back

If we [freely] admit that we have sinned and confess our sins,
He is faithful and just (true to His own nature and promises)
and will forgive our sins [dismiss our lawlessness] and [continu-
ously] cleanse us from all unrighteousness [everything not in
conformity to His will in purpose, thought, and action.]

1 JOHN 1:9 AMP

You knew it was the wrong thing to do. But at that moment, impressing the crowd seemed far more important to you than the consequences of doing such a stupid thing. Now, guilt is eating away at you, and you feel that God is so far away.

There is no justification for wrong. When you do wrong, it hurts God's heart, and you disappoint yourself. Thankfully, the Lord is merciful and forgiving. God says that if you confess your wrong and acknowledge to Him that you are sincerely sorry, then He will forgive you. To God your confessed sin no longer exists. That is God's promise, and He always keeps His promises.

The blood of Jesus is your assurance that your sin, once confessed, is wiped away. God says He will wash you so clean that to Him you look whiter than snow.

YOUR HEAVENLY FATHER PROVIDES AN ESCAPE FROM YOUR MISTAKES. CONFESS YOUR SIN, AND THEN LET GO OF CONDEMNATION.

THE CHANGE WILL COME

So don't get tired of doing what is good. Don't get discouraged and give up, for we will reap a harvest of blessing at the appropriate time.

GALATIANS 6:9 NLT

You have known for a long time that you need to get rid of the excess weight, but things came to a head when you felt pain in your chest. You immediately scheduled an appointment with your doctor. He looked you right in the eye and told you how serious this was. Your doctor gave you a specific diet, exercise instructions, and scheduled your next visit.

God waits for you to ask for His help, and now He is ready to walk you through this lesson in self-control. God provides the doctor to help you with the physical part of the plan. The Lord will train and develop your soul. Your permanent success depends on training your body and exercising your spirit.

Everyday, God's wisdom helps you make the right decisions. The Lord gives you the strength to resist cravings and temptations. Depend on God for success, and you will not be disappointed.

TRUST ALMIGHTY GOD, THE SOURCE OF STRENGTH INSIDE YOU, TO HELP YOU CHANGE BAD HABITS ONE STEP AT A TIME.

UNAFRAID

Wicked people run away when no one chases them, but those who live right are as brave as lions.

PROVERBS 28:1 CEV

Now that you are a Christian, you pray for the opportunity to tell someone about the love of God. And God answers your prayer by sending someone who has the same problem that He delivered you from. You feel the Holy Spirit rising within you and empowering you with the boldness to look the person in the eye. Compassion from the love of God rises in your heart for this person who has lost all hope. You put an encouraging smile on your face and joyfully tell him or her about God's love, saving grace, and mercy. And then, you pray for this person.

Your heart rejoices as the person walks away with a heart of praise as a born-again child of God. Now you know why God said not to be ashamed of the Gospel. It is not a matter of your pride. Rather, it is all about helping others to receive God's love. Once again, you pray with excitement so that you will be ready when God sends someone else your way.

BE CONFIDENT THAT GOD WILL HELP YOU AND HIS PRESENCE WILL SUPPLY THE COURAGE YOU NEED.

ALL THE WRONG PLACES

This is what the LORD says: "Cursed are those who put their trust in mere humans and turn their hearts away from the LORD . . . . But blessed are those who trust in the LORD and have made the LORD their hope and confidence."

JEREMIAH 17:5,7 NLT

Why do we look for human help when trouble comes? Perhaps we find it easier to believe our physical senses. Maybe we feel comfortable with a person who can sympathize with us.

Are you going through a rough time right now and seeking help from someone you know? Your Heavenly Father loves you. Feel free to ask for help from God first, knowing He will not betray you. Nothing is impossible for God to do for you. The Lord loves, protects, heals, and answers your prayers twenty-four hours a day and seven days a week. God is full of wisdom, all-powerful, ever-present, and all yours.

The Lord blesses us with family, friends, and trained professionals to help us. However, pray that God will show you where to go before you seek help and that He will tell that person exactly what to do for you.

———

THE LORD'S PRESENCE IS UNSEEN, BUT HIS LOVE IS
WONDERFULLY MADE KNOWN.

NOT WORTH REPEATING

The tongue is a small thing, but what enormous damage it can do. A great forest can be set on fire by one tiny spark.

JAMES 3:5 TLB

The old saying "Loose lips sink ships" accurately describes the damage that gossip can cause. Gossip is evil and destructive. What benefit is there in spreading rumors that ultimately hurt someone's reputation?

The Bible describes the tongue as a powerful force that can be used to either build up or tear down. Thank God that you are His child and that His Spirit helps you use your tongue in the proper ways: worshiping, praying, reading the Word aloud, and telling others about God's love. Speak only those things that edify others in Christ Jesus.

When you fellowship with God, you learn to say what He says. God is love, and all God does is rooted in His love. As you walk in God's love, you learn to practice restraint when others around you want to gossip. You can rejoice knowing that your mouth speaks with God's love because your heart is full of His Word.

LET GOD HELP YOU TO BRIDLE YOUR TONGUE AND
BUILD LIVES RATHER THAN DESTROY THEM.

NO OTHER NAME

God raised him up to the heights of heaven and gave him a name that is above every other name, so that at the name of Jesus every knee will bow, in heaven and on earth and under the earth, and every tongue will confess that Jesus Christ is Lord, to the glory of God the Father.

PHILIPPIANS 2:9-11 NLT

The Bible says that a good name is better than riches. Sometimes parents research the meaning of a name before they give it to their child. A name can represent anything that celebrates a child's birth, including family genealogy or physical attributes. When you call a person's name, you call forth every aspect of their life—good and bad.

When you call on God, you are calling on all His promises. God immediately hears you, and He will answer you with all His wonderful attributes. The name Jehovah represents the many ways the Almighty God manifests His love for us. God withholds nothing from you—His very presence lives in you. And the Lord gives you the authority to use the awesome name of Jesus to carry out His will.

IN ADDITION TO SALVATION,
YOUR HEAVENLY FATHER GIVES YOU A NEW NAME
(ISAIAH 62:2). WHEN GOD CALLS YOUR NAME,
ANSWER HIM WITH A HEART OF LOVE.

A JOYFUL NOISE

Sing, O heavens, for the LORD has done this wondrous thing.
Shout, O earth! Break forth into song, O mountains
and forests and every tree! For the LORD has redeemed
Jacob and is glorified in Israel. The LORD, your Redeemer
and Creator, says: "I am the LORD, who made all things.
I alone stretched out the heavens. By Myself I made the earth
and everything in it."

ISAIAH 44:23-24 NLT

You love your Heavenly Father with all your heart. Tears of joy run down your cheeks when you remember how loving and faithful He has been. Your heart swells with thankfulness for His grace and mercy. When you pray, you humbly bow your head and knees in reverence to His magnificence and power. But when you are at church with other people, you become self-conscious and feel that all eyes are on you. Your mouth is dry, and you cannot sing. While other people clap their hands and dance before the Lord, your hands hang by your side as if they were made of lead, and your feet feel rooted to the floor.

Jesus Christ came to free you from all bondage. That means you are free from being self-conscious and timid. You can use your voice, hands, and feet to show your love and thankfulness to God in worship.

———

YOUR PRAISE AND WORSHIP EXALT THE LORD.
JOYFULLY GO INTO GOD'S PRESENCE.
HE EAGERLY WAITS.

FROM THE HEART

*One day spent in your house, this beautiful place of worship,
beats thousands spent on Greek island beaches. I'd rather scrub
floors in the house of my God than be honored as
a guest in the place of sin.*

PSALM 84:10 MSG

Do you remember how your heart soared with joy as the pastor and his wife welcomed you as a new member of the church? You were so thankful to have a church family and such a beautiful place to meet with them and God.

Now, a few months later, you are vacuuming, dusting, polishing, and picking up candy and gum wrappers in the sanctuary. Perhaps this is not what you like to do.

No, you did not make a mistake. Obviously, God needs you here. You asked how you could help, and they gave you this assignment. Your Heavenly Father has shown you what He needs you to do.

———

IT PLEASES GOD WHEN YOU WELCOME HIS PRESENCE EVERYWHERE YOU GO. GOD ENJOYS WALKING AND TALKING WITH YOU AS YOU WORK. YOU AND THE LORD CAN HAVE A WONDERFUL TIME OF FELLOWSHIP ANYWHERE AND ANYTIME.

TIME TOGETHER

Upon their return, the apostles reported to Jesus all that they had done. And He took them [along with Him] and withdrew into privacy near a town called Bethsaida.

LUKE 9:10 AMP

Technology is a wonderful gift from God. However, it seems the more advanced technology gets the more stressed out we become. For instance, have you noticed that people are busy talking on a cell phone everywhere you go? In traffic, in restaurants, in church, in school, and in checkout lanes in stores—people are busy handling their lives by phone. Sometimes families are so busy with outside interests that they spend little time together. When they do have an opportunity to relax at home they watch television, surf the Internet, or play video games rather than sit down to a family meal.

If that is an accurate description of your life, then maybe it is time to reset your schedule so that you spend quality time with your family and your heavenly Father. Yield your time to God and allow the Holy Spirit to lead you into His presence whenever He desires.

A SUCCESSFUL, HAPPY LIFE BEGINS WITH PERSONAL TIME WITH GOD. YOUR FELLOWSHIP WITH HIM PROVIDES YOU WITH THE WISDOM, LOVE, JOY, PEACE, AND POWER TO TAKE CARE OF ALL YOUR RESPONSIBILITIES.

ABOVE AVERAGE

If you listen obediently to the Voice of GOD, your God, and heartily obey all his commandments that I command you today, GOD, your God, will place you on high, high above all the nations of the world.

DEUTERONOMY 28:1MSG

You are happy, healthy, and successful— enjoying the good life God has given you. You cannot thank the Lord enough for all that He has done. But deep down you are beginning to feel somewhat dissatisfied, as if you have reached a plateau, but why? You begin to do a lot of soul-searching as you pray and wait in the Lord's presence.

Your humble, sincere heart pleases God very much. Being sensitive to His Spirit leads you to seek answers from Him rather than go elsewhere. Because you love God first and foremost, you immediately look to Him to satisfy the longing in your heart. You know that true contentment comes from pleasing the Lord and not yourself. God has plans for you that exceed the ordinary. And your obedience to Him will cause you to be greatly blessed and enable you to be an even greater blessing to His Kingdom.

GOD'S DESIRES AND PLANS FOR YOUR LIFE ARE BETTER THAN ANY OTHERS. OBEYING THE LORD RESULTS IN AN EXTRAORDINARY LIFE.

THE RIGHT MOVE

In his heart a man plans his course,
but the LORD determines his steps.

PROVERBS 16:9 NIV

A church in your diocese has almost burned to the ground. Volunteers are asked to go help rebuild it, and it would mean having to temporarily move there. As president of the benevolence committee, you immediately decide to raise your hand first. But you feel the Holy Spirit warning you not to do it. You start to raise your hand again, but you feel that same warning not to volunteer.

Just before the members leave early the next morning, you receive an emergency call from a neighbor. Your wife has collapsed at home and has been rushed to the hospital. At the hospital, the doctor explains what happened and assures you that your wife is out of danger, but will need weeks of bed rest.

As you hold your wife's hand, you thank the Holy Spirit who warned you and helped you obey God, in spite of your persistence to do things your own way.

———

NO MATTER HOW HONORABLE THE CAUSE OR HOW GOOD YOUR INTENTIONS, GOD DOES NOT WANT YOU TO MAKE A MOVE WITHOUT FIRST ASKING HIS WILL.

A MADE-UP MIND

For God has not given us a spirit of fear, but of power and of love and of a sound mind.

2 TIMOTHY 1:7 NKJV

You have an important decision to make very quickly. You are still gathering details and reviewing facts. It is not going to be as easy as you thought. Lord, a lot is depending on this decision, and many people are depending on me. And I'm depending on you to tell me what I need to know and what I need to do.

God is pleased that you believe He has the right answer for you. He sees and knows everything. Nothing is hidden from God, and He knows exactly what to reveal to you. With His knowledge and wisdom at your disposal, you will know what is right and true. And because He has given you the mind of Christ (1 Corinthians 2:16), a sound mind, you will not be confused. So rest in God's presence and allow the Holy Spirit to lead you into making the right decision. It will not be hard to do after all.

YOUR MIND MUST BE HEALTHY TO UNDERSTAND AND OBEY WHAT GOD SAYS IS RIGHT.

LET'S GET ALONG

Live in harmony with one another . . . If it is possible, as far as it depends on you, live at peace with everyone.

ROMANS 12:16,18 NIV

Someone swore at you and made an unkind gesture. Several people witnessed it. It would be easy to strike back and get even; but deep within you, the Holy Spirit is speaking the peace of God to your heart.

God sees your wounded soul. As you listen, you hear the Holy Spirit speaking peace to you. Place your feelings in God's hands and trust Him to help you remain calm. Rely on the Lord's strength to help you obey Him in spite of your feelings or the other person's actions. God's love will help you see past the person's unkindness so that you can forgive him or her.

Now, you can walk away in peace with God, with yourself, and hopefully with the one who did you wrong. Your Heavenly Father will restore your dignity and your joy because you chose to be a peacemaker.

GOD WILL TEACH YOU HOW TO BE A PEACEMAKER
SO THAT YOU CAN RESPOND TO PERSECUTION WITH
LOVE INSTEAD OF RETALIATION.

GOD IS WILLING!

*A man with leprosy came and knelt before Him and said,
"Lord, if you are willing, You can make me clean." Jesus
reached out his hand and touched the man. "I am willing," he
said. "Be clean!" Immediately he was cured of his leprosy.*

MATTHEW 8:2-3 NIV

What is your most urgent need right now? Do you doubt that God will take care of it? Probably not, because you know that God loves you and takes wonderful care of you. The Lord will not withhold anything that you need. Now, think about something that you really desire. Do you hesitate to ask God for it because you think that He might consider it frivolous and not give it to you?

Your Heavenly Father promised to supply your needs, and He also promised to give you the desires of your heart because you delight in Him (Psalm 37:4). You are His child. He wants you prosperous, happy, and healthy. You do not have to explain or give a reason for asking Him anything because the Lord already knows that your heart is sincere. So be comfortable and confident when you pray and know that God will not humiliate you or make you grovel. God welcomes you to come, ask, and receive so that your joy may be complete (John 16:24 NIV).

GOD IS READY, WILLING, AND ABLE TO PROVIDE WHAT
YOU NEED AND DESIRE SIMPLY BECAUSE YOU ASK.

A NEW SONG

He has given me a new song to sing, a hymn of praise to our
God. Many will see what he has done and be astounded.
They will put their trust in the LORD.

PSALM 40:3 NLT

After the week you just had, you express thanks
to God for the strength that kept you going.
You finally finished work and are looking forward
to some well-deserved peace and quiet.

"Dear Father, I'm so grateful to have a direct
line to Heaven. I don't know what I would have
done without You. Thank You for Your help," you
pray as you fall to your knees beside the bed. After
awhile, you sense something stirring in your heart.
An old hymn comes to mind, and you slowly begin
singing. The words express your love for God; and
with a thankful heart, you sing it again and again
from the depths of your soul.

Afterwards, time seems to stand still as you
bask in His presence without saying a word. And
suddenly you hear a sweet melody that permeates
the atmosphere of your bedroom. Without a
shadow of doubt, you recognize your Heavenly
Father's voice. You climb into bed, wrapped in His
arms, listening as God sings of His love and joy
for you (Zephaniah 3:17).

THE LORD'S NEW MERCIES EACH DAY GIVE YOU A
REASON TO LIFT YOUR VOICE IN PRAISE TO HIM.

INDEX

REFERENCES

Scripture quotations marked CEV are taken from the *Contemporary English Version*, copyright © 1991, 1992, 1995 by the American Bible Society. Used by permission.

Scripture quotations marked NLT are taken from the *Holy Bible, New Living Translation*, copyright © 1996. Used by permission of Tyndale House Publishers, Inc., Wheaton, Illinois 60189. All rights reserved.

Scripture quotations marked AMP are taken from *The Amplified Bible. Old Testament* copyright © 1965, 1987 by Zondervan Corporation, Grand Rapids, Michigan. *New Testament* copyright © 1958, 1987 by the Lockman Foundation, La Habra, California. Used by permission.

Verses marked TLB are taken from *The Living Bible* © 1971. Used by permission of Tyndale House Publishers, Inc., Wheaton, Illinois 60189.

Scripture quotations marked MSG are taken from *The Message*, copyright © by Eugene H. Peterson, 1993, 1994, 1995, 1996. Used by permission of NavPress Publishing Group.

Scripture quotations marked NASB are taken from the *New American Standard Bible*. Copyright © The Lockman Foundation 1960, 1962, 1963, 1968, 1971, 1972, 1973, 1975, 1977, 1995. Used by permission.

Scripture quotations marked NIV are taken from the *Holy Bible, New International Version*®. NIV®. Copyright © 1973, 1978, 1984 by International Bible Society. Used by permission of Zondervan Publishing House. All rights reserved.

Scripture quotations marked NRSV are from the *New Revised Standard Version* of the Bible, copyright © 1989 by The Division of Christian Education of the National Council of the Churches of Christ in the USA. Used by permission. All rights reserved.

Scripture quotations marked NKJV are taken from *The New King James Version*. Copyright © 1979, 1980, 1982, Thomas Nelson, Inc.

Scripture quotations marked KJV are taken from the *King James Version* of the Bible.

Scripture quotations marked NASB are taken from the *New American Standard Bible*. copyright © The Lockman Foundation 1960, 1962, 1963, 1968, 1971, 1072, 1073, 1975, 1995. Used by permission.

Also available from Honor Books:

Coffee Break Devotions: Cappuccino

Coffee Bread Devotions: Latte

Good Morning God!

Good Night God!

Glimpses of an Invisible God

If you have enjoyed this book, or if it has impacted your life, we would like to hear from you.

Please contact us at:

Honor Books,

An imprint of Cook Communications Ministries

4050 Lee Vance View

Colorado Springs, CO 80918

www.cookministries.com